MW00709518

The Dips and Spreads Guide

Tasty delicious
recipes

THE
DIPS
AND
SPREADS
GUIDE

Xavier Waterkeyn

NEW
HOLLAND

Contents

Dedication

This book is dedicated to you, dear readers, and to my maternal ancestors:

My great grandmother Juana Arcaya de Millian;

My grandmother Matilde Adelaida Millian de Baez; and

My mother Teresa de Jesus Marcelle Baez de Waterkeyn.

I never met my great grandmother or my grandmother, both died long before I was born so I never got to know them.

My mother, I know all too well, and in the year this book was first published reached the auspicious age of 88. Well done, Mother!

I feel nevertheless that it is from *all their collective influences* that I acquired my enjoyment of cooking and my passion for eating. And now I hope, dear reader, that I can pass on some of that enjoyment and passion to you too.

Introduction

Dips and Spreads
A Very Brief History

When you think about dips, what usually comes to mind is the classic party dish in a bowl surrounded by crackers or potato chips of various descriptions or, for the more vegetally inclined, chopped up sticks of carrots, cucumber and celery (also known as crudités).

Dips are essentially thick sauces on steroids (figuratively, of course). Whereas sauces are liquids that accompany and add flavor and texture to other foods, on Planet Dip the emphasis is on the 'sauce' itself and its own flavor and texture. Dips are thick sauces as party foods in their own right. The dipper, whether it's a water biscuit or a stick of bell pepper, is really just a way of transporting the dip into your mouth without getting your fingers dirty. Nevertheless, the dipper is an essential element to the total dipping experience. Spreads are just the thicker cousins of the dip, too dense to thrust a potato chip into, but just right to apply to the surface of bread, toast or those 'low calorie' crispbreads that you buy so that you can pretend that in some mysterious way they are slimming.

Dips are not just party food; they can form the basis of a snack or light meal in and of themselves. I'm sure many of us have often spent many a quality hour relaxing in front of the television, binge watching something or other with a small (or in my case, large) bowl of hummus, taramasalata or some dip that involved cottage cheese and sour cream - or both - and a fresh baguette or disc of Lebanese bread gradually getting torn into pieces, dunked into said dip and then devoured, bite by bite.

Unfortunately, exhaustive research on my part has failed to uncover the historical origin on the dip, perhaps because all the very early cooks were illiterate, and the people who were literate didn't think to write about dips. The word itself in English derives from an old Germanic verb dupjan which was pronounced approximately like 'doopyan' and it meant 'to immerse'. If we wanted to be pedantic about it the modern usage we should really be calling them 'scoops', but I guess that ship sailed long ago.

So, dips themselves are probably very old, their origins lost to antiquity. Sour cream came from Eastern Europe in the late 1800s, but there are soured milks, cream cheeses and yogurt-like cultured products (like labneh) from all over the world that date back many centuries all of which might have formed the basis of some sort of dip. Hummus dates back to the Middle Ages and might have played a role feeding Saladin while he was fighting crusaders in the Holy Land. I'd like to think that Ancient Greeks or Romans were arguing over the finer points of philosophy two thousand years ago while enjoying bread and something that resembled tapenade. This is certainly possible because in a twelve-volume series of books called De Re Rustica (Concerning Country Things) the Roman agricultural writer Lucius Columella mentions a recipe called Olivarum Conditurae (olive and celery spread) which is certainly among the oldest dip recipes that have survived the centuries.

I've included this recipe [on page 167] so that you can have a taste of the ancient world without having to go on a holiday and see ruins. I suggest that you eat some Olivarum Conditurae while spending some quality time in front of the television binge watching one of those excellent BBC historical documentary series about Ancient Greece or Rome.

Dip Etiquette

'Etiquette' is rather an old-fashioned term for the simple courtesies that we observe as part of pretending to be civilized.

Here are the basic rules of dip etiquette:

One: NO DOUBLE DIPPING.

No part of the dipper that has made contact with your mouth should go back into the dip.

Occasionally if you have an especially long crudité or breadstick then you can dip with the end of the dipper that has not made contact with your mouth.

HOWEVER, you should take care that the virgin end of the dipper has not come into contact with your fingers.

Under no circumstance should your fingers or any other part of your anatomy touch the dip in the source bowl.

Two: NO HOGGING

If you have a large appetite for dips, you might linger a little too long over the bowl and cause a dip traffic jam. This situation can be easily avoided with some foresight. The thoughtful host or hostess could provide spoons and small plates so that guests can serve themselves their own personalized selection of dips and eat to their heart's content without interfering with anyone else's enjoyment.

If the dip is almost gone, and if it seems that you'll be the last dipper, the polite thing to do is to ask if anyone else would like some. Usually the answer will be 'no', since people are usually happy to reward someone with the last dip when they were polite enough to ask and to put others first.

Three: NO CONTAMINATION OR CROSS-CONTAMINATION

For health reasons no dips from source bowls should contaminate dips in other source bowls. Lots of dips contain nuts, and some people are SO allergic to nuts that they need medical attention if they're in the same room as a nut. If a host has designated a dip 'safe' for an allergy sufferer, then don't be responsible for careless cross-contamination that might result in someone's hospitalization.

On the part of the guest, if you have any concerns about allergies you MUST inform the host beforehand.

On the part of the host, it's a good idea to keep potentially hazardous dips and non-hazardous dips separate and keep gluten dippers (like crackers and bread) and non-gluten dippers (like potato chips, crisps and crudités) separate. If you're using commercial chips/crisps read the packet carefully to ensure that there are no allergens. You'll usually see a warning paragraph like 'May contain nuts and/or milk products and/or soy products'. Perhaps if things are this fragile it might be a good idea to create separate plates for allergy sufferers or to serve them first, leaving the rest of the guests to serve themselves, knowing that those with special needs have been looked after.

SPECIAL NOTE -

The Broken Chip / Crisp / Cracker Rule

Try as we might and with the best of intentions, sometimes we miscalculate the delicate stresses that we put our crackers under and the cracker breaks off into the dip. The dipper must take immediate action and use another dipper to rescue the fragments from the dip and provide a relatively clean dip for the next dipper.

IS IT A DIP OR IS IT A SPREAD?

Ultimately, the decision on whether a particular recipe that you conjure up is a 'dip' or a 'spread' depends on how you're using it: Are you dunking in (a dip) or dumping on (say, bread)?

The biggest deciding factor on whether it's a dip or a spread will be the texture you end up with.

Most dips can be thickened or thinned by varying base ingredients, and to some extent on the temperature of the dip or spread at the time that you use it.

Colder dips are, as a rule, thicker or more viscous than warm ones.

It's entirely in *your* power to control texture, and with experience you'll get just the consistency *you* want.

The main exception to this rule are the seed and nut butters, which are really too thick and pasty to every be suitable for dips so, by default, end up being classified as spreads. However, there's nothing stopping you from using a seed or nut butter as the basis of a dip, if you throw enough cream cheese, mascarpone or even vegetable puree at it and blitz it up in a food processor.

Who knows what serendipity might result from a little experimentation?

Dip and Spread Fundamentals

Dips and spreads come under several broad categories depending on the base ingredients.

DAIRY DIPS

These are dips based on sour creams, yoghurts and cheeses, or a combination thereof. These dips often include the addition of mayonnaises that modify texture and flavor, even though mayonnaise is not a dairy product.

SEAFOOD AND PÂTÉ

Pâté is just the French word for 'pasted' as in 'turned into a paste'. Theoretically you can turn lots of things into a paste but the term has become essentially synonymous with spreads made from liver - usually chicken or goose - and usually involve some cream and butter too. However, there are other pâtés based on fish, usually with cream cheese, sour cream, mascarpone, crème fraiche or mayonnaise as a base on which to build.

The many potential varieties of taramasalata are also seafood and can have a bread base (page 92) or a gluten free, mashed potato base (page 151).

BEAN DIPS

These dips are based on beans and other legumes (such as peas) as the base. They also include the dizzying array of hummus (which is based on chickpeas).

VEGETABLE DIPS

These dips can have a starchy vegetable base, such as pumpkin or sweet potato, but they also include 'fruity' vegetables such as eggplant (baba ganoush), olive (tapenades), tomato (salsas) and avocado (guacamole). Come to think of it, nearly all the 'vegetables' I've mentioned are botanical fruits, with the exception of sweet potato, which is a tuber. But calling these 'fruit dips' would have given you a totally wrong idea.

SWEET STUFF

Sweet spreads are rather a mixed bag of different types and techniques although most of them are either dairy-based. They are included here for those who wish to indulge their sweet tooth and because they're fun to make with, and for, children. Sweet dips are surprisingly rare, but I've included a few ideas here to get you started.

SEED AND NUT BUTTERS

These butters are basically oily seeds and nuts that have been ground to a thick paste. They are mostly sweet too, but there are also savoury options mainly built around miso (page 114) so you'll find those ideas back in the Bean and Legume section. Peanut-butter spreads are technically bean spreads too but are, as far as most people are concerned, nut butters, so let's not quibble. These butters are usually 'spreads' but can be used to enhance the flavors of dips as the basis for dips in their own right if thinned out a little with a cheese, cream or vegetable puree.

THE ART OF
PREPARATION

The Golden Rules of Dips and Spreads

Dip making isn't exactly rocket science. Dips are some of the easiest things to make, they often don't involve cooking, and they are very forgiving even if you don't follow the recipe to the letter.

Unlike baking, where ingredients are carefully weighed and measured, dips are an inexact science.

They're really more of an *art*.

Golden Rule 1:

Don't Sweat the Small Stuff.

DIP MAKING IS MORE OF AN ART THAN A SCIENCE.

A dip recipe should be considered more like a set of broad brushstrokes rather than a strict, paint-by-numbers plan. It's this inherent ease and flexibility of the dip that makes making dips with children a great way to introducing them to cooking and to exploring new flavors and textures. These recipes are perfect for trying out a taste exploration, especially the foods of other cultures, with children (and with grown-ups with a childlike sense of fun). It's true that children (and a lot of grown-ups!) can be picky eaters, but the right dip or spread is an excellent and relatively cheap way to broaden your experiences and develop a person's palate.

Given that taste is a subjective thing one cook's over-spiced chili is another's under-spiced bland – *it's therefore crucial with dips and spreads that you taste as you go.*

Golden Rule 2

Taste as You Go.

Add extra amounts of ingredients in small batches so that no single ingredient overwhelms any others.

Sometimes it's a fine line between adding enough of one ingredient, especially a herb or spice, and too much. So go a little at a time, especially with some of the stronger flavors.

Nonetheless, be willing to experiment with variations on a theme.

Have a small pot of boiling water on the go. Get a spoon and taste the dip as you create it, sampling for flavor and texture, then clean the spoon in the boiling water after each taste so that you don't contaminate the dip as you're making it.

Remember also that many flavors take time to mature and several hours of refrigerating a dip will allow flavor components to blend.

The potential flavor variations are *virtually endless,* so experiment and have fun.

Golden Rule 3

Dips Are an Art.
Presentation is everything.

Feel free to experiment with presentation by adding finishing sprinkles of anything from mild chili, paprika, black pepper, to mixed herbs.

Color and texture don't have to be limited to the food, so use good-looking serving bowls too to showcase the brilliant dips you'll be making. After all, in many cases dips are something you serve when entertaining, so it helps to present your dips to your guests with a little showmanship and flair. With any luck, the photographs and suggestions you'll find in these pages should go a long way to giving you ideas and inspiration to make all those thick but delicious pastes look, as well as taste, outstanding.

EQUIPMENT AND QUANTITIES.

THE BASIC DIP-MAKING EQUIPMENT INCLUDES:

◊ Scales for measuring your quantities

◊ Bowls: sturdy for mixing and pretty for serving

◊ Spoons for measuring and serving

◊ Spatulas for scraping the maximum dip from your cooking equipment

◊ Storage containers for those rare times that there'll be any dip left over, or if you're planning to freeze.

The only specialty must-have is a food processor, for pureeing, mixing and blending - a process collectively known as blitzing.

If you don't have a food processor, a standing blender or even a stick blender will do the job in many cases. For nut butters, you NEED food processor, in order to provide that extra bit of oomph.

The recipes in this book all aim at producing about 500 grams or about a pound of dip or spread. This is about two to three times the quantity of the amount that you'll find in a standard commercial container for dips that you'll find in a supermarket.

WHY THIS MUCH?

Well, for starters, as easy as dips are, if you're going to go to the trouble to make a dip, you might as well make a reasonable amount of the stuff to justify the clean-up. Also, making the stuff at home is often going to cheaper than buying the store-bought dips. If you're planning a party that involves more than about ten people you're going to need larger quantities anyway, and if you have growing children in the house, especially physically active teenagers, you're going through a ton of food so the more the merrier. In the end, you need to decide for yourself how much you want or need. For a smaller size, simply halve the quantities quoted.

Finally, many dips, especially the vegetable dips, are freezer-friendly and improve with flavor after freezing, so you can always have some on hand if you prepare enough beforehand.

BEFORE WE GET STARTED

PREPARATION TIMES

Please note that unless I state otherwise, assume a preparation time of somewhere between five and fifteen minutes. People vary hugely in how long they take to cook stuff and *preparation times are extraordinarily unreliable*, since they don't include preparation and clean up - some cooks are MUCH messier than others and have never learned the art of 'clean as you go while waiting for that other job to get done', which saves a huge amount of time.

Good cooking *requires* time for ingredients to come into their own, time for flavors to mature and blend.

The good news is that this maturation of flavors doesn't usually require *your* time. If you're just a little organized then in only a few minutes you're just setting everything up. Dips are among the easiest and quickest things you

can do in the kitchen but most of them will need time in the refrigerator to fulfil their potential.

MISE EN PLACE

One of the first things you ever learn in cookery school is 'Mise en Place', which is the French way of saying 'Put in Place'. One of the best tips that anyone can ever give you when it comes to cooking is to have everything in place every ingredient pre-measured and ready-to-go; every bit of equipment clean and set up before you start cooking. The recipes are written with Mise en Place in mind. If you have everything ready the whole process of cooking is easier and more enjoyable.

COOKING

Some dips require some cooking, perhaps of beans (if you don't want to use cans) or perhaps of vegetables. This is no big deal. Some nut and seed butters require roasting. This is no big deal either. But rather than bore you with endlessly repeating the same instructions in recipe after recipe, it's easier to just give you all the cooking tips that you'll need in one place. In the case of this book, that one place is in the appendix: Cooking for Dips and Spreads, starting on page 199. There you'll find all you'll need to cook legumes without going crazy, or to get the most out of vegetables through the process of slow caramelization.

STORAGE

At the other end of the process is storage. Most dips will keep in the refrigerator for about a week. Those dips that lend themselves to freezing with last a couple of months. My storage preference is glass, those containers with a rubber-ring seal, because they don't take on the flavors of what they contain. However any good-quality plastic container, especially if it's designed for freezing, is fine too.

WARNING:

If you're storing a seafood dip then after four hours at room temperature you should throw it out. With any luck it will be so delicious that there won't be any left after four hours anyway.

ON THE USE OF SALT

Saltiness is very subjective and not everybody likes a lot of salt. It's an easy condiment to add and because it's soluble its effects are immediate, but it's IMPOSSIBLE TO REMOVE. In any case a lot of the ingredients in dips and dippers like potato chips are already salty, so there's no need to add more salt.

GET YOUR BASE RIGHT AND EVERYTHING ELSE SORTS ITSELF OUT

A recurring theme that you'll find here is the idea of bases. You create a base dip around a combination of creams, cheeses, vegetable purees or nut pastes, and then you build on them according to your particular preferences. With this approach of bases to which you can add additional ingredients you can generate *hundreds of different variations* without the need to have a recipe book that's hundreds of pages long, repeating the same themes over and over again, and writing out lots of different recipes that might only be different because of an ingredient or two.

Dairy Delicious

Dairy Dips - The Basics

The recurring theme you'll find with dairy dips is that they're variations on four ingredients:

Sour cream

Yoghurt

Soft cheeses

Mayonnaise

These basic four bases are then mixed in various proportions depending on the tastes and textures that you like and blended with various flavorings.

The variations are endless. You can get a lot of mileage simply out of mixing your cheeses - there are literally *thousands* of cheese varieties even within the realm of cows' milk cheeses which you can add to your bases to enhance and blend flavors at your leisure. For those allergic to cow's milk, goats milk and sheep's milk offer alternatives, although their lower fat content tends to make their choices as dips more limited and confined to additional touches, rather than bases. Brebis (sheep) and Chevre (goat) cheeses are not as common, somewhat more expensive but people with allergies are used to this sort of stuff.

I've found that the most practical way to mix dairy-based dips is with a stick blender, since the ingredients are all soft and using a stick blender saves a lot on washing up.

Mayonnaise

Legend has it that mayonnaise was invented by Napoleon's personal chef, but who really knows? Mayonnaise (usually considered a sauce) isn't *usually* considered a dip or a spread, but this wonderful invention is, in fact, *all three*.

In Belgium, French fries are often served with mayonnaise as a dunking dip, especially with cracked black pepper. In the Netherlands a lighter version of mayonnaise, with less oil and more water and vinegar or lemon juice, is called *Fritessauce* sauce for fries.

Mayonnaise has a bad reputation as being difficult to make, but in fact it's pretty easy. You've just got to have a knack for it or acquire one through a little practice.

Basic, Classic Mayonnaise

INGREDIENTS

◊ 500 ml (approx. 1 pint) oil

◊ 2 eggs

◊ water

The oil can be any neutral or mild tasting oil, like vegetable oil, safflower, sunflower or grapeseed oil. You can also use olive oil, as long as it's one of the lighter ones, but most people find olive oil (even the lighter varieties) to be much too thick.

It's important that the oil be cold, as warm oil won't blend properly. Use cold or cool bowls too. Feel free to refrigerate the oil. If the oil solidifies a little, just wait a little until it warms up enough to liquify again. You can blend more flavored oils with lighter oils too. Experiment!

You can use whole eggs or just the yolks. It's entirely a matter of personal preference. The eggs should be cold too.

The standard ratio of egg to oil is one yolk to 250 ml (1/2 pint) of oil.

METHOD ONE

Get a stick blender.

Get one of those tall containers that usually come with the stick blenders and place the eggs in.

Blitz the eggs for a few seconds, on a low speed if you have a variable-speed blender.

You can also use a hand mixer with a strong bowl, or a stand mixer. If you want to build up your forearm muscles, you can also use a whisk.

Add a small quantity of oil. No more than say, 30 ml (1 oz) and blitz again until the mixture has thickened.

While blitzing, gradually pour in oil a little at a time pausing now and again to let the oil thoroughly blend into the gradually growing pool of mayonnaise.

Continue this process until you've used up all the oil and the mayonnaise is done.

I know what you're thinking. You're thinking, 'That doesn't sound too hard!' *But the risk is in adding too much oil at once*. Now with some experience you can do this:

METHOD TWO

Put in the eggs add all the oil at once in a tall container.

Put in the stick blender. You make sure that the business end of the stick blender reaches to the very bottom of the container.

Turn it on. Resist the urge to move the blender up and down too much. Keep the blender still and allow the blender to do its work and the mayonnaise makes itself because it self-regulates how much oil mixes in at a time.

NOTES:

If the mayonnaise is too thick, you can pour in a little water. You'll see the mixture turning paler. Again, this is a matter of taste. I personally like a thick mayonnaise, since it's so often comes into contact with watery foods like vegetables anyway and that tends to thin it out.

Adding additional elements also thins out the mayonnaise so my advice is not to add water or lemon juice in the beginning. *Make it thick to start off with* and take it from there. A thick mayonnaise gives you a lot more control over the final texture of your dip.

STORAGE NOTE

Mayonnaise, or any dip with mayonnaise in it, doesn't freeze very well. You can try, but I wouldn't recommend it.

Mayonnaise just on its own will, however, keep for several weeks in the refrigerator without a problem.

The storage life of a dip that's already mixed with mayonnaise in it is no longer that a week. It's not that the mayonnaise goes off, so much that it's an emulsion - an inherently unstable mixture of oil and water - and after a

while it begins to separate, especially when exposed to heat. Also, because it's made of raw egg, it needs to be kept well sealed so that it doesn't become a breeding ground for bacteria.

Mayonnaise Variations

All of these variations work well as spreads but they all make great dips that you can dunk hot French fries into. Why should Belgians have all the fun?

COCKTAIL SAUCE/DIP

Add 20 ml (2/3 fl oz) of ketchup or tomato sauce to the mayonnaise. The addition of finely chopped semi-dried tomato instead of ketchup makes for a rather more sophisticated experience than that of the usual cocktail sauce.

GARLIC

A little minced garlic goes a long way and turns your mayonnaise into aioli. Roast Garlic (page 210) is a more unusual variation.

HORSERADISH

Use only a little horseradish to give your mayo a nice Germanic kick.

LEMON

Instead of water, or in addition to water, you can use lemon juice. Note that this will make the mayonnaise much paler and thin it out. You can also use lime juice and this lime variation works well with salsa dips.

MUSTARD

Mustard is usually a welcome addition to mayonnaise. In fact, some consider it compulsory. Because there are so many different types of mustards the one you select will have a profound effect on the character of the mayonnaise. For 500 ml (about 1 pint) of mayonnaise, a teaspoon of mustard might be enough, but feel free to add as much as you want. Grainy Dijon works well as does sweet Bavarian and any of the mild mustards. Hot mustard is not for the faint of heart. If you're using dry mustard powder be very cautious, a little goes a long way.

SUGAR

Many people like their mayonnaise a bit on the sweet side but I think it's probably a good idea to forgo adding sugar to mayonnaise until you know what you're committing to when you use it as an element in another dip. I *personally* wouldn't like a sweet mayonnaise in a crab dip, but this is a matter of taste.

TARTARE SAUCE

Add a pinch of pepper (white or black) and salt to taste and 1 tablespoon each of the following:

◊ Finely diced pickles

◊ Capers

◊ Grainy seed mustard

Throw in a small, diced Spanish onion too if you feel the need.

Once the tartare sauce is made this perennial seafood favorite also works well as a dip in its own right with the addition of canned fish of your choice. The mix should be about 1/3 sauce to 2/3 fish. Make sure that the fish is well drained and remove any bones before adding the tartare sauce.

REMOULADE

This is a more elaborate version of the tartare theme. The particular remoulade you end up with depends on your particular family recipe. Flavors you can incorporate in your remoulade in addition to or instead of the ones in tartare sauce include:

◊ Anchovies

◊ Cayenne pepper

◊ Curry

◊ Horseradish

◊ Paprika.

Only add a little of each flavoring at a time. Anchovies in particular can quickly dominate, if not overwhelm, other flavors.

VINEGAR

Like mustard, vinegar is another one of those ingredients that many people feel is a mayonnaise 'must'. Just like lemon or lime juice, vinegar is acidic and will affect the consistency and color of the mayonnaise, so add it in small quantities at the end and check as you go. The huge variety of flavored vinegars available provide many opportunities to experiment. Just remember that if you're using colored vinegar some of that color will affect the end result. Go light on the red wine vinegars unless you want your mayonnaise with a pinkish tinge.

WASABI

This popular Japanese condiment works really well in mayonnaise, and not just with Japanese food. Make sure that the wasabi is well blended so that you don't get small lump in your mouth all at once and the hot surprise that goes with it. Having said that, when the Japanese mix wasabi into a dipping sauce they often allow for little lumps so that there's always that thrilling possibility of getting a little jolt of spicy surprise. Do whatever works for you.

EGG AND CURRY DIP

This isn't so much a mayonnaise variation as a proper dip with only mayonnaise as a base. Take about 200 ml (8 oz) of mayonnaise and stir in a tablespoon full of a curry paste/powder of your choice. Now add about 6 or 8 boiled eggs that you've either roughly chopped or roughly blitzed in a bowl. The result is a high-protein dip that's moreish and works with any bread but really well with dark rye or pumpernickel in particular. Feel free to add some freshly ground black pepper or finely sliced chives for an extra kick or two.

Classic Dairy Dip Base

In case you missed my point earlier, rather than bore you with dozens of recipes that basically repeat the same information over and over, I'm going to provide you with a simple base, and you can create whatever dip you like from this fundamental mixture. From here you can explore to your heart's content using the suggested variations.

INGREDIENTS

◊   200 g (7 oz) mayonnaise (page 30)

◊   200 g (7 oz) of sour cream

METHOD

Hand blend the mayonnaise and the sour cream until thoroughly combined. The texture should be as silky smooth as you can make it.

VARIATIONS TO THE BASE

◊ Substitute cream cheese for the sour cream. If you're going to do this make sure that the cream cheese is at room temperature and blitz it in a food processor before adding any other ingredients. Cream cheese needs to be a little warmed, aerated and whipped up before it's soft enough to be used in a dip and this is best achieved in a food processor. The result will still be thicker than the classic base.

◊ Substitute fresh goat's cheese for the sour cream. This is a suitable alternative for those who are allergic to cow's milk. Make sure that the goat's cheese is at room temperature before blending, and it's probably best done in a food processor.

◊ Substitute crème fraiche, Labneh (page 66) or Greek yoghurt for the sour cream. This can be hand-blended, but the result will be more fluid and lighter than with sour cream so you might want to go lighter on the mayonnaise for this base variation, unless you like a very fluid dip. It all depends on how thick your starter mayonnaise is.

◊ Substitute mascarpone cheese for either the mayonnaise or the sour cream. Most people, if they think of mascarpone at all, only ever think of tiramisu, but it's actually a great base cheese for dips. It has the weight of a thick labneh, but without the tang and it isn't as fatty as crème fraiche.

Classic Dairy Dip Ideas

Cold Blue Cheese Dip

TO THE CLASSIC BASE ADD:

◊ 120 g (3 1/2 oz) of crumbled blue cheese

◊ 10 g (1/3 oz) of chopped chives

◊ 10 g (1/3 oz) of chopped parsley

Spicy Jalapeno Dip

TO A BASE MADE FROM CRÈME FRAICHE AND MAYONNAISE ADD:

◊ 4 spring onions (scallions), finely chopped

◊ jalapeno peppers, finely chopped, to taste

◊ 4 teaspoons of ground black pepper

◊ 1/2 teaspoon of Cayenne pepper (optional)

Parsley and Almond

TO THE CLASSIC BASE ADD:

◊ The leaves from a medium bunch of Italian or continental parsley, roughly chopped.

◊ 4 spring onions (scallions), finely chopped

◊ 45 ml (1 1/2 fl oz) of lemon juice

◊ 4 or 5 cloves of garlic (minced raw or Roasted - page 210)

◊ 120 g (4 oz) of slivered almonds, either blanched or Roasted (page 218)

Romanian Garlic and Tomato

TO 450 ML (15 FL OZ) OF A BASE OF 100% SOUR CREAM ADD:

◊ 1 bulb of garlic

◊ 4 medium tomatoes, deseeded and finely chopped

◊ 4 teaspoons of mustard

The traditional Romanian recipe calls for raw garlic, but you can give the roasted stuff a try (page 210). Otherwise start with a small amount of raw garlic and add to taste.

The tomatoes need to be deseeded or there'll be too much liquid in the dip and it'll go runny. So, cut the tomatoes into quarters and cut out or scoop out the seeds before chopping the tomatoes. If you have a garden, or even some flower pots and a balcony, I suggest planting the seeds. You can never have enough tomatoes.

Warm Fennel Dip

TO 450 ML (15 FL OZ) BASE OF 100% SOUR CREAM ADD:

◊ 2 large or 4 small fennel bulbs, roasted then thinly sliced (page 212)

◊ 30 g (1 oz) of caramelized roasted onions (page 215)

◊ 4 Roasted garlic cloves (page 210)

◊ 4 tablespoons lemon juice

◊ 3 tablespoons grated parmesan cheese

◊ 3 teaspoons fennel seeds

If you're roasting your vegetables fresh, just combine all the ingredients and hand blend, then hand blend the sour cream at room temperature. If you're using roast or caramelized vegetables that you've prepared earlier, combine them then warm them in a microwave before adding the sour cream. The vegetables need to be warm, not hot, or they'll make the sour cream too runny. The sour cream needs to be at room temperature. If cold it'll cool down the vegetables too much. If you find this mixture too chunky, feel free to blitz it a little with a stick blender before serving.

If you have everything else but the fennel and you're in a hurry you can slice the fennel then sauté in a little oil until golden and tender before continuing with the rest of the preparation.

French Onion Dip

I should make a special mention of this classic dip. The best versions of French onion dip aim to emulate the rich complexity of French onion soup in a thick, creamy base. There's nothing even remotely French about this dip. Legend has it that it was invented in the 1950s in Los Angeles.

Storage: Refrigerated for up to a week. Keeps frozen for 3 months.

Preparation Time: About 5 minutes but MUCH longer if you haven't already prepared some Caramelized Onions beforehand.

INGREDIENTS

◊ 50 g (2 oz) of Caramelized Onions (page 215) or more to taste.

◊ 200 g (7 oz) of Mayonnaise (page 30)

◊ 200 g (7 oz) of sour cream

◊ 1 teaspoon of chopped chives

METHOD

Hand blend the mayonnaise and the sour cream until thoroughly combined. The texture should be as silky smooth as you can make it.

Fold in the onion, adding more onion if you want a stronger flavor.

Add salt and pepper to taste.

Serve at cool room temperature with a sprinkle of the chopped chives.

Some people add half a teaspoon of beef stock powder or half a beef stock cube to the dip to add a more of an umami note. Other umami enhancers include a dash of Worcestershire sauce or even the tiniest touch of Marmite, Promite or Vegemite.

If you're in a rush, and you haven't got caramelized onions, then the classic quick fix is to blend a packet of single-serve French onion soup powder into the mayonnaise and sour cream mixture. Having said that, using your own, homemade mayonnaise and caramelized onions produces a *far* superior product.

Brie Dips
& Camembert Dips

Brie and camembert are the most famous and most easily available of the white, soft-rind French cheeses. They're similar, but not identical. Brie has cream added to it during its making and the result is a smoother, creamier cheese. Brie is the milder of the two. Camembert has a much sharper flavor. Traditionally brie is a much bigger cheese, but baby brie is now the same size as camembert a wheel that's around at the most, about 12 cm (5 inches) and weigh in at about 200 to 250 g (7 to 8 oz).

The following recipes are for warm dips. Feel free to use either cheese and experience the differences in flavor and texture.

Preparation Time: 15 - 20 Minutes

Garlic, Thyme and Conserve
Brie / Camembert Dip Spread

INGREDIENTS

◊ 1 wheel of brie or camembert

◊ 1 clove garlic, finely sliced OR 1 or 2 cloves Caramelized Garlic (page 210)

◊ 2 sprigs of thyme (or 1/2 teaspoon of dried thyme)

◊ 4 teaspoons of jam, marmalade or conserve of your choice

METHOD

Pre-heat oven to 180°C (350°F).

Take a small baking dish and place cheese within. Ideally it would be one of those small, round terracotta baking dishes that are just big enough to hold the cheese.

Make a long slit in the middle of the cheese and then another one so that you form an 'X'.

Insert or push in the garlic into the slit.

Sprinkle the thyme over the top of the cheese.

Spoon the conserve over the top of the cheese.

Cover the whole thing in foil.

Bake for about 8 - 10 minutes if the cheese is at room temperature, or 15 minutes if the cheese is coming straight from the refrigerator.

Serve hot to warm.

NOTES:

If you don't have a baking dish, then the next best thing is to get a large square of foil and a square of baking paper. Place the baking paper on top of the foil, then place the cheese in the centre and proceed as above. Wrap everything up and bake the cheese within the paper / foil wrapping on a baking tray. Serve directly from the opened foil once you've cooked it.

Even when baked this dip is still a little too firm to dip a cracker or a potato chip in directly. I suggest it works better as a warm spread and that you dig into it with a butter knife and then spread on toasted bread of your choice.

VARIATIONS

The recipe says 'jam, marmalade or conserve of your choice' - here are some particularly nice pairings that work with the thyme and garlic:

◊ chili jam

◊ cranberry sauce

◊ fig jam

◊ raspberry jam

◊ sweet orange marmalade

◊ seville (bitter orange) marmalade.

YOU CAN ALSO ADD A TABLESPOON OF:

◊ dried cranberries

◊ currants, raisins or sultanas

◊ ground, toasted nut of your choice, like, say, almond, hazelnut or walnut.

◊ sundried tomatoes, finely chopped

◊ a small sprig or half a teaspoon of dried, ground rosemary either with or instead of the thyme.

Baked Brie with Artichokes

USING THE METHOD ABOVE, BUT IN A LARGER BAKING DISH ADD:

◊ 200 g (7 oz) of artichoke hearts (thoroughly drained of brine or oil or whatever they've come in - pat dry with paper towels if you have to) finely chopped

◊ 4 teaspoons of grated parmesan cheese

◊ 4 teaspoons fresh Italian parsley, finely chopped

Chili Con Queso

This Mexican warm dip simply means 'chili with cheese'. The base dip is super easy to make, and then all you do is add additional flavorings of your choice.

INGREDIENTS

◊ 30 g (1 oz) butter

◊ 1 teaspoon (more or less) of chili powder

◊ jalapeno chilies, finely chopped, to taste

◊ 240 g (8 oz) of sour cream

◊ 240 g (8 oz) coarsely grated cheddar of your choice

METHOD

In a heated saucepan, sauté the chili powder and chilies in the butter for about 30 seconds to a minute in order to release the chilies' flavors.

Stir in the sour cream until heated.

Stir in the cheddar cheese until melted.

Serve warm.

VARIATIONS

Add any one or a combination of the following:

◊ 4 cloves of caramelized garlic (page 210), mashed up.

◊ shallots (scallions) or caramelized onion (page 215), finely chopped

◊ 10 g (1/3 oz) chopped, fresh coriander (coriander)

◊ 1 large diced tomato, seeds removed and diced, or 45 ml (1 1/2 fl oz) of tomato salsa

Cream Cheese Dips

Cream cheese, much beloved by cheesecake makers everywhere is, on its own, too heavy to make a dip … BUT …

Cream Cheese Base Dip

INGREDIENTS

◊   400 g (12 oz) cream cheese

◊   100 g (3 1/2 oz) mayonnaise

METHOD

Get the cream cheese out of the refrigerator and cut into large chunks.

Throw the cream cheese and mayonnaise into the food processor and blitz.

After a minute or so in the food processor the mechanical blitzing both warms and aerates the cream cheese and incorporates the mayonnaise, making the whole mixture lighter and fluffier.

Taste for texture and add more mayonnaise until you get the texture you want.

It's pretty bland so at this point you can add ingredients, *to taste*. Here are some suggested flavor combinations:

◊   chili, garlic and paprika (smoked paprika works well too, but you'll have to go easier on it than for the non-smoked variety)

◊   roasted red peppers

◊ garlic and dry-fried, chopped bacon

◊ sweet chili sauce and Thai basil

◊ satay made with sweet chili sauce, peanut butter, ginger, coriander and lemongrass paste

◊ caramelized Fennel (page 212) and chives

◊ dill, red onion and smoked salmon

◊ nchovy and white onion (go easy on the anchovy!)

◊ Refried beans and corn

◊ Sautéed spinach and artichoke. Make sure that the artichoke is well drained. If using artichoke preserved in oil, then sauté the spinach in a couple of tablespoons of the artichoke oil

◊ Roast Pumpkin (page 213) and cinnamon

◊ Pizza sauce and pepperoni

◊ Spring onions and roast chicken (with or without the roast chicken skin).

Naturally, you can use sour cream instead of mayonnaise. I suggest a light sour cream for this one, as cream cheese is already so full of fat that a light sour cream should lift the dip up, make it lighter and add a nice tang too.

The neutrality of cream cheese also lends itself beautifully to sweet dips.

Feta, Ricotta and Cottage Cheese Dips

The special, crumbly, sour character of feta cheese doesn't really lend itself to blitzing in a food processor at least in my not-so-humble opinion. Nor do I think it really combines well with other cheeses, except maybe ricotta and cottage cheese. The same feta dip made from cottage cheese or ricotta will be a much milder, sweeter dip. The cottage cheese version of the same dip will be less fatty than if you're using the other cheeses.

Either way, the best way to make a feta-based, cottage cheese-based or ricotta-based dip is to start with a base:

White Soft Cheese Base

INGREDIENTS

◊ 400 g (13 oz) feta, cottage cheese or ricotta

◊ 45 ml (1 1/2 fl oz) of light olive oil

◊ 20 ml (2/3 fl oz) lemon juice (optional)

METHOD

Mash the feta and the olive oil in a bowl, using a fork, but just enough so that it smooths up a bit, without losing its crumbliness.

Now stir in the flavorings with a fork.

Suggestions

Feel free to try both the feta and the ricotta variations and compare them and see which you like more.

To the above base mixture add and blend to make:

Feta and Date Dip

◊ 90 g (3 oz) dates, finely chopped
◊ 60 g (2 oz) toasted pine nuts
◊ 60 ml (2 fl oz) honey
◊ 1 teaspoon of finely grated lemon zest

Lemon Garlic Feta Dip

◊ 2 teaspoons crushed garlic
◊ 2 teaspoons finely grated lemon zest

Avocado and Feta

◊ 1 large, smashed up avocado
◊ handful of drained, sliced black Spanish olives

Basil and Sundried Tomato

◊ 10 g (1/3 oz) of basil, finely sliced

◊ 3 or 4 pieces of semi-dried tomato, finely sliced

Tirokafteri

Recipes for this classic Greek dip vary from region to region and family to family. Here's your starter and you can take it from here:

INGREDIENTS

◊ 200 g (8 oz) feta

◊ 200 g (8 oz) Greek-style yogurt

◊ 1 tablespoon olive oil

◊ 1 teaspoon lemon juice or a good vinegar

◊ 1 red capsicum (red pepper) without the seeds, either fresh, roasted, canned or preserved in oil.

METHOD

Mash all the ingredients except the red pepper, in a bowl with a fork, until it forms a thick paste that's slightly grainy.

Blitz the red pepper with a food processor or stick blender until it forms a paste.

Blend the red pepper into the rest of the mixture.

Refrigerate for about an hour and serve cold.

Serve with parsley or oregano leaves as decoration, or both.

Labneh / Laban - Strained Yoghurt

Many cultures throughout the world have come upon a common idea take the local yoghurt and strain off the excess whey to make something new a fresh, spreadable cheese. In Central Asia, they call it chakka or suzma. In South Asia, it's called kulhar and is often made from water buffalo yoghurt, which is a little hard to get in most supermarkets in the West. And in the Middle East, it's called labneh or laban. While you use yoghurt as an addition to or substitute for sour cream or mayonnaise in any dip recipe, in general, yoghurt is too thin and runny to make a good dip on its own. So, you'll need to make labneh, which is super easy.

METHOD FOR MAKING LABNEH

Get a clean linen tea-towel, cheese cloth, muslin or any other cloth suitable for fine straining. Make sure that the cloth is well rinsed and hasn't the slightest residual odour of washing detergent or fabric softener on it.

Get a bowl and put a bowl strainer on top of it.

Line the strainer with the cloth.

Place 1 kg (1 quart) of full fat, unflavored yoghurt into the cloth-lined strainer.

Cover the top with cling wrap.

Place the whole thing in the refrigerator for 24 to 48 hours. During this time the wonders of gravity will do their work and the excess liquid whey will drip out of the yoghurt and into the bowl.

Test the strained yoghurt for its texture after the first 24 hours. The longer you leave it, the thicker and cheesier it will get.

Feel free to keep the watery whey if you like. It has a lot of nutritional goodness. You can mix it into thick-shakes or smoothies or you can use it instead of milk in a variety of recipes.

NOTES:

You can also use one of those coffee makers that use filter paper for the same result. Make sure that the equipment is really well cleaned though because otherwise your labneh will smell of coffee.

You can also just wrap the yoghurt in a cloth and hang it from a tree. I would only do this in cooler weather though, somewhere where the local wildlife won't get to it. The disadvantage to this method is that you'll also lose the whey.

Even on its own, labneh makes a lovely spread, just add a little salt if you're going to use it for savoury dishes, then form it into golf-ball size balls and then keep them preserved in olive oil OR use the labneh to make:

Labneh Hummus

Using the hummus recipe, substitute half or all of the tahini with labneh. The result will be a much lighter dip. If you want to restore some of the sesame flavor, put in a teaspoon or two of sesame oil into the mixture.

Topped Labneh Dips

In the Middle East, labneh is served by placing it on a serving plate, then using a variety of different toppings. The topping IS NOT mixed into the labneh. That way dippers can mix in toppings with as much or as little labneh as they want.

While the simplest topping is an elegant splash of oil you can also use any of the toppings suggested for Hummus (page 106) and you can also try the following ideas:

◊ Olive Tapenade (page 165)

◊ crushed pistachios, sesame seeds, fresh mint and pomegranate for a splash of color

◊ basil, chives and Roasted Pine Nuts (page 218).

◊ za'atar - A Middle Eastern dried herb mixture - the exact recipe of which depends on where you come from - but which can be purchased from specialist Middle Eastern grocers. If you can't get za'atar you can try a mixture of equal quantities of lightly toasted, thyme and sesame seeds with a touch of sumac to taste.

Tzatziki

This classic Greek cucumber dip is easy to get right as long as you remember to get the excess moisture out of the cucumber.

INGREDIENTS

◊   500 g (approx. 1 lb) of labneh or plain Greek-style yoghurt

◊   1 large cucumber, peeled, seeds removed and finely chopped

◊   4 garlic cloves, pressed

◊   Juice of 1/2 a lemon

◊   60 g (2 oz) or so of fresh dill, finely chopped

◊   Salt and pepper to taste

◊   Parsley for garnishing

METHOD

Take the cucumber in your hands and squeeze out excess moisture. Feel free to use a cheesecloth if you like or, if you've thought a little ahead of time, you can put the cucumber in a bowl first, with a bit of salt, and wait an hour. The salt will leach a lot of fluid out of the cucumber, which is then much easier to squeeze.

Combine all the ingredients in a bowl and blend together with a fork.

Serve cold.

VARIATIONS

◊   Ttalattouri the Greek Cypriot version of tzatziki includes a dash of oregano, the Greek oregano called rigani.

◊ Maast o Khiar, the Iranian version of tzatziki, uses just labneh or yoghurt with cucumber and dried mint as a flavoring.

◊ Raita: hold the lemon juice and dill, but add instead 30 g (1 oz) chopped fresh coriander, 30 g (1 oz) chopped spring onions, 2 teaspoons ground coriander and 2 teaspons ground cumin. This is actually best made the day before or at least a couple of hours before in order to give enough time for the coriander and cumin to release their goodness. Raita is traditionally used as a dip for a variety of dishes and the yoghurt is supposed to act as a way of taking heat away from the mouth if you've had an overdose of chili. I personally have never found it to be very effective for this, but it's delicious, so who cares?

◊ Raita often incorporates mint as well, in which case you might just want to blitz everything and end up with a dip that's a rather pleasant, minty green.

◊ Another common variation is coconut and banana raita, in which the labneh or yoghurt is mixed with thin slices of banana and a small amount of shredded coconut, (raw or slightly toasted). Again, this is reputed to take the heat away from a tongue unaccustomed to too much chili.

◊ Tarator: this Balkan variation is traditionally a soup but can also be a dip. It includes ground walnut and tahini, so add these to taste.

NOTES:

Using labneh instead of Greek yoghurt will result in a thicker dip, but let the dip settle a little first because the labneh will leach out more fluid from the cucumber and will thin it out a bit. If you still don't like the consistency, feel free to add a very small amount of the cucumber juice back into the dip, a little at a time, until you're happy with it.

Hot Cheese Dips

Using a very simple dairy base you can make any number of different hot cheese dips. Let's make life easy on ourselves!

INGREDIENTS

◊ 1 can of evaporated milk (about 350 ml or 12 oz)

◊ 4 teaspoons corn starch (make sure it's corn starch if you want to be gluten free)

◊ 240 g (8 oz) of cheese of your choice just make sure that it's a cheese that melts well. Feel free to mix and match cheeses. Just make sure that the total quantity doesn't exceed 240 g (8 oz).

METHOD

In a saucepan on a gentle flame start heating the milk.

Add the corn starch until it's completely dissolved. I like to dissolve the corn starch in a bowl with a little water, using my finger until I end up with a thin paste that has no lumps in it then throwing the mixture in. Don't worry about the water, it will evaporate away.

Keep stirring.

Add the cheese or cheeses. Depending on the texture of the cheese you might want to crumble it or grate it first. This will help the cheese melt into the milk base. Blue cheese tends to crumble. Firmer cheeses are better off grated.

Keep stirring. Don't worry if the mixture is lumpy and thin. As the cheese melts and the corn starch dissolves changes will occur.

Magically, at about the 10-minute mark, the mixture will suddenly and noticeably thicken.

Since different cheeses melt at different temperatures don't stress if one cheese melts while the other doesn't. Just stir until you have a consistency you like.

On the off chance that the mixture becomes too thick, feel free to add a *little* water or white wine.

Serve when thick and hot or warm.

FLAVORS THAT WORK:

◊ 50 / 50 blue cheese and cheddar

◊ 75 / 25 gruyere and parmesan

◊ 50 / 50 gruyere and edam

◊ 50 / 50 gruyere and gouda

◊ 50 / 50 gouda and edam

◊ 50 / 50 gouda and provolone

◊ 50 / 50 havarti and port salut.

These are just some suggestions. Let your imagination and a spirit of adventure be your guide.

OTHER THINGS YOU CAN TRY:

◊ Stir with a sprig of fresh rosemary instead of, or in addition to, a spoon. Remove the rosemary at the end of the cooking process.

◊ Add a small amount of aniseed or dill seed.

◊ Add a small splash of hot sauce.

◊ Add a pinch of chili, paprika or cayenne pepper, right at the end as a decorative garnish, sort of like the way that baristas dust a cappuccino with chocolate powder, except maybe be a little careful with the chili and cayenne.

GARNISHING AND SERVING IDEAS FOR DAIRY DIPS

The general rule-of-thumb for garnishes is that they should:

◊ be edible

◊ be one of the ingredients in the actual recipe or at least complimentary to those ingredients

◊ be made up of the nicest looking ingredients you can find

◊ be of contrasting color to the main dip.

How does this work in practice?

Say, for example, you're using spring onion in a recipe. Pick out the best-looking spring onion from the ones that you're going to use in the recipe then slice it into thin rings. Use the green part, because that contrasts nicely with the predominantly white or pale color of the dip.

Because dairy dips are white or off white, you're better off serving them in dark bowls.

The subtle flavors of dairy dips are best appreciated with a very neutral dipper like water crackers or white bread. Dark breads or dark crispbreads tend to overwhelm dairy dips.

I've chosen the seafood dips to follow on from the dairy section, because they're mostly built around a dairy base. To this base, you just add the seafood of your choice.

Seafood Dips

Something Fishy

Seafood dips DO NOT STORE WELL. They should be done relatively quickly and on the spot and refrigerated until the moment of serving. Fortunately, you don't have to store seafood dips because, while seafood isn't to everyone's taste, the people who like it really like it so there won't be any leftovers.

Seafood Dip Base

INGREDIENTS

- ◊ 250 g (8 oz) cream cheese softened and at room temperature
- ◊ 250 g (8 oz) sour cream OR crème fraiche

METHOD

Blitz until thoroughly mixed. I find that a stick blender is usually best for this.

NOTES:

Other dairy products you can use either singly or in combination are:

Greek-style yoghurt or Labneh (page 66)

crème fraiche

mascarpone cheese

If you don't add anything to this base it will keep in the refrigerator for up to two weeks, but it usually doesn't last that long because hungry mouths tend to make short work of it within a short period of time.

Sour cream will make the dip tangier but thinner. mascarpone or crème fraiche will make the dip milder in flavor, but thicker and richer. If you want the thickness of mascarpone or crème fraiche but with a little more tang, then a splash lemon juice or even a caper or three is the way to go.

Feel free to add some mayonnaise too if you like the added silkiness it imparts.

A Word About Crème Fraiche

Crème fraiche works well in all dairy dips as a substitute for sour cream. It's milder in flavor but its high fat content gives it an extra level of lusciousness.

You can buy it in the store, but it's also super easy to make.

Crème Fraiche

METHOD

Add 20 ml (2/3 fl oz) of buttermilk for every 250 to 300 ml (around 1/2 pint) of heavy cream or double cream that is any cream with a fat content of over 45%.

In a container that won't react with acidity (that is to say, plastic, glass or ceramic) mix the buttermilk and the cream together thoroughly.

Cover the container with a lid to stop air getting in.

Cover the container with a tea towel or put it in a dark place at room temperature for anything from 8 hours to 24 hours depending on what 'room temperature' means to you. The warmer the room, the less time you should leave the crème fraiche out. Over that period of time the buttermilk culture will do its chemical magic and turn the heavy cream into crème fraiche. Leaving this overnight usually works in most cases.

You'll know it's done when you try it and you like the yoghurt-like tang.

DO NOT DOUBLE DIP WITH YOUR SPOON because otherwise bacteria from your mouth will contaminate the crème fraiche and spoil it. In most cases I suggest trying it only ONCE after about 8 to 12 hours.

Refrigerate for an hour before using it in a dip.

IMPORTANT NOTE ON USING FISH FOR DIPS

In most cases I strongly recommend using canned or tinned fish or shellfish.

Get fish in oil where possible, rather than in water or brine, because oil-preserved fish mixes better in the dip. Make sure to drain the fish of oil so that the dip doesn't become oily.

If the fish is in water or brine, make sure it's thoroughly drained so that the water doesn't dilute the dip or make it runny.

Make sure that you remove any bones or spines or in some cases even scales, skin and the stray fin or two. We just want the flesh.

Decide on the texture you want beforehand. If you want a smooth paste it's OK to just add the fish, herbs or vegetables all at once and just blitz away to your hearts content. If you want a chunkier dip just chop up your ingredients in any way that you like, and blend them into the dip base with a fork.

Seafood Dip Ideas

Once you have your dip base, the sea's the limit! Here are some quick and easy ideas to get you started. Just add the ingredients below to the dip base.

Smoked Clam Dip

Add the smoked clams from 2 tins (each 85 g or 3 oz for a total of 170 g or about 6 oz). Add a splash or Worcestershire sauce if you like. You can do the same thing with the relevant shellfish to make smoked mussel dip and smoked oyster dip. Serve with finely sliced chives.

Cold Crab Dip

Add 200 g (approx. 7 oz) of crab meat and 1 finely diced Spanish or red onion. Some people like to throw in a little garlic salt in too. The same technique works to create cold lobster dip. A dash of paprika works well with these dips too.

Hot Crab Dip

This works best with crème fraiche and cream cheese because the crème fraiche doesn't split. To the crab dip recipe above add 500 g (1 lb) of cheddar cheese and bake uncovered in a ceramic or earthenware dish at 170°C (350°F) for about 45 minutes to an hour until you get a nice brown crust on top. Serve hot. You can also make hot lobster dip in the same way.

Smoked Salmon Dip

Add 200 g (7 oz) of finely chopped smoked salmon and 60 g (2 oz) of finely chopped dill. This also works with the relevant fish to create smoked trout dip and smoked mackerel dip. Smoked mackerel is usually bought whole, so you'll have to work a little to remove the flesh, but it's worth it. Some of you might also like to add some finely diced dill pickle to taste, or some finely chopped capers.

Tuna Dip

Ignore the base dip for this one. Just add 300 g (10 oz) of canned tuna meat to 200 ml (7 oz) of mayonnaise and 1 finely diced Spanish onion, and add cracked black pepper to taste. This also works with salmon to make salmon dip. I prefer tuna or salmon IN WATER for these ones as oily fish plus mayonnaise is a bit of an overkill of fat. Just be sure to squeeze the fish of excess moisture so that it's relatively dry when you add it to the base. Serve with chives, dill or finely sliced spring onions. Wasabi works well too and, if you're feeling daring, a teaspoon of finely grated parmesan cheese.

Taramasalata

Leaving behind cheese, cream and mayonnaise bases we come to one very special dip, one of my favorites. Taramasalata is the quintessential Greek dip and although is proper name is 'taramasalata' the 'taramosalata' spelling is common too. And while some of the store-bought brands are very good they don't compare to the delights of the home-made stuff.

We're dealing with the salted roe or eggs of the grey mullet, striped mulled, carp, cod or herring. You'll find it in some of the better fishmongers or the more cosmopolitan delicatessens. You can find it colored bright pink, but you can also get it in yellow. If you can't get tarama, your fishmonger might be able to get smoked ling or pollack roe, though you might want to soak the roe in water first to take any overpowering smoke edge off first and drain thoroughly before use. I suggest finding a Greek fishmonger or even a Greek grandmother for advice on the specifics in your area.

INGREDIENTS

◊ 240 g (8 oz) of tarama or smoked fish roe

◊ 240 g (8 oz) of the sponge (the white bit without the crust) of fresh or slightly stale white bread

◊ Juice of half to 1 lemon

◊ half a white onion, finely grated

◊ extra virgin olive oil to taste, but you'll probably need at least 100 ml (3-4 oz)

◊ Black pepper and Italian (flat-leaved) parsley for decoration

METHOD

If you're using very stale or dry bread then pour cold water on it and let it soak for literally 1 second then drain the excess water out and squeeze the sponge so that it's moist but not wet and certainly not soaked wet.

Blitz the tarama, bread, lemon juice and onion until you have a smooth paste.

Gradually add olive oil until you have a consistency and flavor you like.

Serve cold with parsley and black pepper to taste.

NOTES:

Taramasalata is very much a matter of taste, so if you you're uncertain for starters use less tarama in the beginning and add more until you find a level of that salty, fishy goodness that works for you.

GARNISHING AND SERVING IDEAS FOR SEAFOOD DIPS

The classic garnishes for seafood dips are:

◊ dill

◊ parsley

◊ zest or thin slices of lemon or lime

◊ very thin slices of red or Spanish onion.

All of these add color and flavor without clashing.

Blue or green bowls work well with seafood dips because they're 'sea colored' although if you have bowls the color of beach sand these would work well too. Don't underestimate the power of color-coding, especially if you're serving a variety of different dips to a wide variety of people. At a glance your guests would be able to avoid the seafood dips if seafood isn't their thing.

Because of their strong flavor, seafood dips work well with strongly flavored dippers, so a good light or dark rye bread, or a dark crispbread or dark cracker works well with seafood dips. Pumpernickel is one of the great breads but too crumbly to use as a dipper. However, if you're using the dip as a spread then any of the smoked fish dips with pumpernickel is an excellent flavor paring.

Pâté

A TOUCH OF FRANCE

In a book dominated by cheeses, creams and vegetables, and even totally vegan options, I nevertheless felt that our journey into the wonderful world of dips and spreads would be incomplete without mentioning dealing with pâté too and since it doesn't really fit anywhere else, I thought I'd give it its own little section.

Pâté recipes can be extraordinarily elaborate. Some recipes require slow cooking in a water bath or baking in a special ceramic dish, but since I'm trying to make your dips and spreads adventure fun and doable without a lot of equipment that you might not have, I'm providing you with a very simple, basic recipe that you can then tweak to your heart's content.

INGREDIENTS

◊   240 g (8 oz) chicken livers

◊   125 g (4 oz) butter

◊   125 ml (4 oz) heavy cream

◊   1 small brown onion finely chopped

◊   1 clove of garlic

◊   1 or 2 teaspoons of a aerb or spice of your choice (see below)

◊   45 ml (1 1/2 fl oz) of an alcohol of your choice (see below)

◊   clarified butter or ghee for covering

METHOD

Clean the livers by removing any sinew or any other bits that look discolored and then set the livers aside.

In a really hot pan, add a few tablespoons of butter. If you're using raw onion then cook the onion until transparent first, this shouldn't take long. If you're using caramelized onion then just place it in. Immediately add the liver and the garlic and sauté the livers until just done. This is easy to determine. Make sure that they're well browned on the outside then just cut one open and if it's still juicy, keep cooking. Either way liver doesn't take very long to cook. It shouldn't be more than a couple of minutes. The liver should still be a bit springy to the touch. Add the cream and remaining butter and the herb of your choice and give everything a good stirring. Only cook now until the cream and butter are warm. Place the whole lot into a food processor, add your alcohol of choice and blitz the mixture.

When well blitzed, transfer the still warm pâté into a nice earthenware or ceramic dish, or one of those sealable glass jars. Smooth out the surface and cover the pâté with a shallow layer of clarified butter, or ghee. If you don't crack the butter layer, this will keep for weeks and the flavors will slowly improve too.

Refrigerate and always serve cold.

NOTE:

You're under no obligation to use as much butter or cream as the recipe calls for. If you do, you'll get a very smooth, soft pâté. If you up the liver and go lower on the butter and cream, you'll end up with a thicker, more spreadable pâté.

Ghee is easy to make. Just put some butter in a saucepan and gently melt it until all the yellow butterfat is on top and all the white milk solids have collected at the bottom. Pour off the butterfat from the top and save it; that's the ghee.

You can also do this pâté with duck liver and goose liver if you can get it. Since these livers are larger you'll maybe need to cut them up a little before the sauté.

Herb, Spice and Alcohol
(and Even Fruit)
Combinations that Work

◊ Grand Marnier and black peppercorns

◊ Cointreau and black peppercorns

◊ Brandy and sage

◊ Sherry, ground allspice and thyme

◊ Sherry and orange zest

◊ Cognac and cranberries (you can use Craisins dried cranberries that you've then pre-soaked in the cognac and then finely chopped)

◊ Armagnac and prunes (Really! You'd be surprised)

◊ Port and caramelized fig [see note below]

◊ Port and caramelized pear [see note below]

NOTE:

Caramelize the pear and fig in the same way that you'd do Caramelized Garlic (page 210), only leave out the olive oil. Just slow bake the fruit in foil and let the heat do the rest until they're browner and richer. You'll be able to tell by the smell.

GARNISHING AND SERVING IDEAS
FOR Pâté

In keeping with the general principles of garnishes, pâté should be garnished with an ingredient it already has, for example, thin slivers of orange zest, caramelized fig or caramelized pear for the applicable pâté above.

Earthenware or terracotta bowls work best with pâté because of that earthy feel that pâtés have.

Pâté is best served with a fresh, crusty French bread like a Baguette or an Epis. Resist the urge to cut the bread too far in advance as it tends to dry out when sliced. Either cut or tear the bread as you go or give your guests mini French rolls and let them work it out for themselves.

LEGUMES AND BEANS

BY ALL MEANS

Beans and other legumes, such as peas and lentils, have the advantage of lending themselves into pastes of the right consistency for both dips and spreads.

A wonderful thing about legumes is that they contain a lot of essential amino acids, the building blocks of protein. Humans need 9 essential amino acids to make the proteins that they need. The bad news is that legumes tend to lack the essential amino acid methionine.

The good news is that grain or seed or nut-based dippers, like breads and crispbreads, are rich in methionine, so when combined in a tasty dip, you get rather a lot of good nutrition. Some dips, like Hummus (page 106), already combine the legume (chickpea) and the seed/nut (tahini) so they are complete proteins in themselves.

The good news is also that legumes are also rich in vitamins, minerals and in fibre, which is wonderful for keeping both you and your gut healthy.

And the good news continues in that legumes are cheap and easy so they're idea for experimenting with. If you have a cookery failure with beans you won't have wasted as much money as, say, if you have a cookery failure with smoked salmon.

All bean dips are essentially the same. The foundation is a base made from a paste of the cooked bean. For the foundation of preparing you bean bases, look in the Cooking for Dips section on page 109.

Classic Hummus

Hummus, Hummous, Hoummus, Hoummous ...

No matter how you spell it, Hummus bi Tahini is one of the great dips that also works wonderfully as a sauce

served with chicken or lamb. Chickpeas never tasted so good.

STORAGE:

Refrigerated for up to four days but must be covered with a thin layer of oil at the top.

Preparation Time: About 20 minutes.

INGREDIENTS

◊   1 x 400g (about 1 pound) can of chick peas

◊   3 cloves of garlic

◊   juice from 1 lemon (more if desired)

◊   45 ml (1 1/2 fl oz) tahini

◊   90 ml (3 oz) extra-virgin olive oil (more if desired for serving)

◊   30 g (1 oz) finely chopped parsley

METHOD

If you wanted to be a purist, you'd take about 200 g (about 1/2 a pound) of dried chickpeas, pre-soak them in about a litre (2 pints) of water overnight. Then boil them for about 1 1/2 hours until they're actually edible having produced about 450 to 500 g (about 1 pound) of finished, cooked chickpeas. Or you could forego the soaking and wait 4 hours to cook them. But really, who has the time? In any case canned chickpeas are perfectly fine for the purposes of making hummus.

Take the can of chickpeas and put them in a colander and rinse them thoroughly. You might notice that some of the chickpeas have an outer skin that's flaked off. Remove these skins if you have the time and the inclination because they have a chemical in them that affects the nutritional value of the chickpeas and removing them makes them more digestible. I've said this elsewhere, but I can't guarantee that you're reading this book cover-to-cover, no matter how entertaining or fascinating my prose might be. This is the sort of thing that you can quietly do in front of the television or while you're chatting with a friend because it requires almost no attention or brain power. Removing the skins does somewhat improve the texture, in my humble opinion.

Let the chickpeas drain so that there's no excess moisture.

Place lemon juice, garlic, tahini and a little of the oil in a food processor and pulse until well blended. Add the chickpeas and gradually add more oil and blend until you have a smooth paste and a flavor that you like.

Transfer dip to a serving bowl. Use the parsley, sprinkled on top as a garnish and use some extra olive oil to drizzle on the top. Refrigerate. Hummus is best served cold.

VARIATIONS

Even though basic, classic hummus is one of the great dips known to humankind, it also lends itself to flavorsome variations.

YOU CAN:

◊ Use another herb instead of parsley, such as basil. Just be careful if you're using a very strongly flavored leaf such arugula / rocket, because it can easily overwhelm the other flavors.

◊ Use lime juice instead of lemon juice. You might need twice as much lime as lemon though, because it's a milder flavor.

◊ Finish with a sprinkle of smoked paprika.

◊ Finish with a dollop of Harissa (page 141).

◊ Use half olive oil and half avocado oil. The result is more expensive but delicious.

◊ Garnish with chopped jalapeno peppers.

◊ Garnish with Beetroot Dip (page 161).

◊ Garnish with Caramelized Onion (page 215).

◊ Garnish with Roast Capsicum (page 210).

◊ Garnish with Roast Garlic (page 210).

◊ Add some Roast Carrot (page 209)

◊ Add some Roast Pumpkin (page 213)

◊ Add some Roast Sweet Potato (page 213)

◊ Garnish with semi-dried tomato.

◊ Garnish with a roasted nut of your choice (page 218)

OTHER VARIATIONS

You can substitute any equivalent amount of canned or frozen white bean for the chickpeas including cannellini beans, navy beans or baby lima beans but at this point you're moving into non-traditional hummus territory. However, you'll still maintain the basic character of hummus if you use tahini, garlic and lemon as your flavor profile. Mung beans make a nice hummus too and some people find them more digestible than chickpeas.

Although we in The West are more accustomed to the large, pale tan chickpea, most of the world's production is in the smaller desi variety, that can range in color from beige to green to black. These will also produce hummus, but in a variety of different shades and subtly different flavors.

Chickpeas, like many legumes, can be sprouted. A hummus made from sprouted chickpeas is likely to be crunchier and less smooth than from cooked chickpeas, and you might have to add more tahini, oil or even a touch of yoghurt to add creaminess, but it might appeal to some palettes and some people find it more digestible too.

Other Hummus Variations

TO THE CLASSIC MIXTURE ADD:

◊ Cauliflower: 100 g (3 1/2 oz) of Caramelized
  Cauliflower (page 212).

◊ Pea: substitute half the chickpeas (200 g or 7 oz) for
  an equivalent amount of cooked peas. This hummus
  maintains the character of both legumes. Feel free to
  substitute the garlic in the classic recipe for a couple
  of tablespoons of chopped mint too if you like.

◊ Kale: 100 g (3oz) of red or green kale. Prepare the
  kale by stripping the leaves from their stalks (you
  don't have to be neat about it), then blanching the
  leaves for 30 seconds to a minute in boiling water.
  The easiest way to do this blanching is simply by
  putting the leaves in a bowl and pouring boiling
  water over them from water you boiled in an electric
  kettle. Easy! And no pots or pans to wash up. When
  the leaves are limp, drain them and let them dry,
  then blitz them in to food processor along with the
  hummus.

◊ Moroccan Hummus:
  1 small Spanish onion diced
  1 tablespoon tomato paste
  1 tablespoon of turmeric
  1/2 teaspoon each of ground cinnamon, ground
  coriander and ground cumin
  a dash of chili powder or Cayenne pepper

◊ Spicy Orange Hummus: to the Moroccan Hummus
  recipe above add
  juice of 1/2 an orange
  1 tablespoon orange zest
  1 teaspoon mustard
  1/4 teaspoon each of ground ginger and paprika

Note on Texture

Some people like a thick hummus, some people like a thin hummus. The more tahini you use, the thicker it will be, but the end result will have a stronger sesame flavor.

The general rule too is that the less olive oil you use, the thicker it will be. Some people like to use a small amount of water to thin their hummus out, but I tend to feel that using water tends to sacrifice the balance of flavors. Using another legume, such as cannellini in addition to chickpeas, can help thin your hummus out without sacrificing flavor. As usual, feel free to experiment.

Note on Storage

What limits the shelf life of hummus is the addition of lemon juice and garlic, since the acid in the lemon and the sulphur compounds in the garlic (especially raw garlic) will start to react with the chickpea/bean base as soon as you add them. If you want to make your hummus last longer, just make the basic hummus without lemon or garlic and add these ingredients a few hours before serving long enough for the flavors to blend in.

The Wonders of Miso

Miso is, quite justifiably, considered a superfood. Its origins are lost to time. Traces in clay pots dating back at least 12,000 years indicate that the Japanese have been making some form of fermented foods since before there even was such a thing as Japan. The Chinese applied their own fermentation principles to soy products and then introduced them to the Japanese in an era when Buddhism made creative vegetarianism a thing.

This salty paste is the product of cooking soybeans, grinding them up, and then fermenting them with salt and koji, a fungus known to science as *Aspergilius oryzae*. In case you're feeling squeamish about fungus, remember that the yeast so beloved by beer drinkers and bread eaters is also a fungus. Because few people have koji lying around the house and are unprepared to invest the months required to ferment miso to maturity, miso belongs to that group of food making that is 'do not try this at home'. Lucky for us, it's becoming much more freely available in supermarkets although you'll need to go to a Japanese specialty grocer to find some of the more exotic varieties. It's rich in protein, vitamins and minerals and is used in a huge variety of recipes, including sauces, marinades and dips and of course, miso soup misoshiru.

Aside from an interesting additives to oriental-style dips, in Japan it's used also as a spread, but it also combines well with nut pastes to make unusual and highly nutritious butters.

During the centuries of its development miso has evolved into some interesting varieties, depending on additives, which include:

Genmai brown rice

Gokoku five grain: barley, foxtail millet, proso millet, soy and wheat

Moromi unblended koji

Mugi barley

Taima hemp seed

However, the main varieties are:

Akamiso red miso

Hatchomiso grain and gluten free miso

Shiromiso white miso

Generally, the redder or browner the miso, the less grain and less gluten it has.

Use it with care as its high salt content might not appeal to all palettes or nutritional needs.

MISO DIPS AND SPREADS

Because of its strong flavor and the fact that miso is not something that will appeal to every palette, miso dips and spreads are best prepared in small batches. They work well with crudités.

Pea Miso

INGREDIENTS

◊ 200 g (7 oz) cooked peas, drained and cooled

◊ 20 ml (2/3 fl oz) mayonnaise

◊ 4 teaspoons miso of your choice

◊ 4 teaspoons chopped spring onions

◊ 1 teaspoon wasabi paste (optional or to taste)

METHOD

Blitz peas, mayonnaise, miso and wasabi (if using) until you form a smooth paste.

Stir in the spring onions with a fork. Serve chilled.

VARIATIONS

Substituting the same quantity of peas for another bean or vegetable and using the same method as with the Pea Miso you can make:

Edamame Miso

Use edamame (cooked and removed from the pods) and add a tablespoon of chia seeds (black or white) and a small dash of olive oil.

Cauliflower Miso

Use Caramelized Cauliflower (page 212) and add a tablespoon of toasted sesame seeds (page 218) and a small dash of sesame oil.

Eggplant Miso

Use with Caramelized or Roasted Eggplant (page 207) and add a tablespoon of tahini and 2 cloves of Caramelized Garlic (page 210).

Pumpkin Miso

Use Caramelized or Roasted Pumpkin (page 213) and add 2 cloves of Caramelized Garlic (page 210),

1 teaspoon of cumin OR nutmeg and a small handful of Toasted cashews, pine nuts or walnuts (page 218).

AND, FOR THE ADVENTUROUS, THERE'S ALSO:

Kimchi Miso Dip

Blitz one part miso and three parts of kimchi with small amount of a neutral oil.

White Miso Dip

Mix one part white miso with three parts of Greek-style yoghurt and add a dash of honey and maybe a little garlic and sesame oil.

Tofu and Miso Dips

For exploring a range of completely vegan dipping options you can create a base mix of three parts silken tofu and one part miso. Make sure that you use silken tofu it's texture is somewhat similar to Greek yoghurt or labneh. From this base you can let your imagination run wild. Adding tahini, lemon and garlic to taste will give you a hummus flavor profile, adding avocado, lemon and tomato will give you a high protein variation on guacamole. Semi-dried tomato and olive oil will give you a harissa feel.

Feel free to use silken tofu in any recipe that requires fresh cheese, cream, mayonnaise or yoghurt to get a vegan option.

Then adjust how much miso you want in order to control the saltiness and umami flavor profile.

I Can't Believe It's Not Guacamole

Let's face it, avocadoes can be expensive, but with a little imagination and some fava beans you can get something that approximates the flavor and texture of guacamole at a fraction of the price.

INGREDIENTS

◊ 400 g (14 oz) of cooked fava beans, with their thick white outer skins squeezed off

◊ 120 g (4 oz) of mayonnaise (page 30)

◊ juice of 1 lemon

◊ 1 large tomato, seeds and pulp removed and medium diced

◊ 1 teaspoon of parsley finely chopped for decoration

◊ salt and pepper to taste

METHOD

Blitz the fava beans, lemon juice and mayonnaise with a stick blender until the texture is smooth with maybe a few bits of bean that still chunk the mixture up somewhat.

With a fork, blend in the tomato so that its well mixed without breaking up in the dip.

Season to taste. Sprinkle parsley on top. Serve chilled.

Notes

If you're still missing that avocado taste you can use some avocado oil at the blitz stage as well as at the end as a finishing oil.

Vegan Mayonnaise

In spite of my general misgivings about the anti-nutrient properties of beans, especially those contained in their skins and the need to remove them, my vegan friends assure me that I should mention aquafaba.

Aquafaba literally 'water of the bean' is the reduced, leftover cooking water from beans or legumes. Chickpea aquafaba being especially useful for many purposes.

The consistency of aquafaba is similar to that of egg whites as are its frothing and binding qualities. As such, aquafaba is a favorite of vegans, and lends itself to a number of dishes for which you'd usually need egg whites including vegan meringues, pavlova, mousse, 'butter', 'buttercream', 'cheese' and even marzipan. But those are recipes for another time and place. For now, let's talk about vegan mayonnaise. This is essentially a mayonnaise made without eggs.

STORAGE:

Refrigerated for up to week. Longer if you're lucky, but this vegan mayo is a little more unstable than the traditional stuff.

Preparation Time: About 20 minutes.

INGREDIENTS

◊ The aquafaba 'juice' of 1 can of chickpeas about 60 ml (2 oz)

◊ 1/8 of a teaspoon of cream of tartar

◊ 180 ml (6 oz) of oil

METHOD

Mix the cream of tartar and the aquafaba with a hand-mixer or stick-blender until you've whipped the stuff and it forms soft peaks. This should take about 4 to 6 minutes.

Using the same method as you would for 'normal' mayonnaise, gradually add the oil, not too much at once, making sure that you thoroughly incorporate the oil before you add any more. As the mayonnaise builds up it keeps its white creaminess, but it never quite achieves the same texture as classic mayonnaise. It's more like a mayonnaise whip.

NOTE:

Make sure that the aquafaba and the oil are cold when you're making mayonnaise. This helps create the right mixture.

Don't add more than 180 ml (6 oz) of oil for every 60 ml (2 oz) of aquafaba - this keeps the ratio to not more than 3 to 1. Any more oil and the mayonnaise risks separating.

If you're going to incorporate dry flavorings like mustard powder or even sugar, it's best to add these at the beginning, before you add the oil. If you're going to add liquids, like teaspoon of lemon juice or vinegar, add these at the end, after the oil is fully incorporated.

Vegan mayonnaise lends itself to the same myriad variations as regular mayonnaise.

Mexican Bean Dip

This is a dip for those who really love Mexican food and who want a vegan dip that is just as good warm as it is cold. Have it on its own or use it in the spectacular Layered Mexican Dip (page 128).

STORAGE:

Refrigerated for up to four days but must be covered with a thin layer of oil at the top. Freeze for up to 3 months.

Preparation time: About 20 minutes.

INGREDIENTS

- ◊ 1 can (about 400 g) of 4 bean mix OR refried beans
- ◊ 1 large brown onion, finely diced OR 2 heaped tablespoons of Caramelized Onion (page 215)
- ◊ 2 cloves of garlic, minced
- ◊ 1 teaspoon ground cumin
- ◊ pinch of chili flakes (optional)
- ◊ 45 ml (1 1/2 fl oz) of diced chipotle OR jalapenos OR sauce made from these chili varieties
- ◊ juice from 1 lime or 1/2 a lemon
- ◊ olive oil for frying
- ◊ avocado oil for flavoring

METHOD

Heat a pan on medium heat until warm. Add oil.

Fry onions until soft or add caramelized onion.

Add cumin and garlic (and the chili, if you're using it) and cook for about a minute, just to take the edge off the raw garlic and to bring out the essential oils in the spices.

Place beans, chipotle/jalapenos, citrus juice in a food processor. Add the items that you've been frying.

Blitz until well combined and until the texture works for you. Add some avocado oil if serving on its own and if you like the flavor.

If serving warm, return it briefly to the pan and serve in the pan or transfer to a smaller sauce pan. A cast iron one looks pretty if you have one or you can use an oven-proof enamel or glazed earthenware dish.

Serve with shaved or grated cheese of your choice.

VARIATIONS

If you can't get four bean mix then three bean mix works just as well too.

If you can't get three bean mix then any red or brown bean can work too.

Layered Mexican Dip

This isn't so much a dip recipe as a fun way present dips whose flavors complement each other. It makes for a nice way of serving a large amount of dip if you've got a lot of people to feed.

You'll need a clear glass bowl that can contain just over 2 litres (4 pints) of dip. Feel free to halve the quantities if you don't need so much dip.

INGREDIENTS

◊ 500 g (1/2 lb) of Mexican Bean Dip (page 124)

◊ 500 ml (1 pint) sour cream (or use a vegan sour cream substitute)

◊ 500 g (1/2 lb) of Guacamole (page 151)

◊ 200 g (½ lb) of diced tomato

◊ splash of lemon juice or lime juice

◊ 200 g (½ lb) of grated cheese of your choice (or use a vegan soy cheese)

◊ Italian parsley, roughly chopped, to garnish

METHOD

Layer dips in alternate layers within the bowl. How you do this specifically is up to you.

I recommend dividing the dips into two halves and layering like so:

Top garnish parsley

Cheese layer

Tomato layer (with a splash of citrus juice)

Avocado layer 2

Sour cream layer 2

Bean dip layer 2

Avocado layer 1

Sour cream layer 1

Base layer of Bean Dip.

Feel free to do whatever you want, but this works best when the layers are distinct and contrasting.

Serve with a large serving spoon so that people can serve themselves their portions on individual plates.

VARIATIONS

Include some diced avocado in the top layer.

A thin layer or two of well-drained, sliced black Spanish olives would also work well, between the layers of sour cream and either the guacamole or the bean, for maximum contrast.

Serve in a shallow dish, rather than a deep one, for smaller quantities.

Serve in individual clear dessert glasses, for a more refined touch.

A Word About Lentils ...

This oft-neglected legume isn't as eaten as often as it could be in the standard Western diet, but it's extremely versatile. The dips you make from lentils will depend on the type of lentil that you use, each having a different flavor and texture.

DO NOT USE the smaller red, orange or yellow lentils as they dissolve in cooking and are best used in mashes, soups and that perennial favorite of vegans, dahls.

This leaves us with whole bunch of other varieties from the humble brown and green lentils to the black beluga, lenticce verdi, marrow, petite castillo, petite estoria, Spanish pardina and the puy among others.

In short, ANY legume-based dip will work by substituting the original bean or pea with a thick puree made from your blitzed lentil-du-jour. But for the sake of a recipe that's a little different and shows off the lentil to its best advantage try the African Spiced Lentil Dip on the next page.

African Spiced Lentil Dip

- ◊ 400 g (2 lbs) of cooked lentils pureed in a food processor.
- ◊ 1 carrot, small diced
- ◊ 1 medium onion, diced
- ◊ 60 g (2 oz) of unsalted butter or ghee
- ◊ 1 teaspoon ground coriander
- ◊ 1 teaspoon ground cumin
- ◊ 1 teaspoon ground ginger
- ◊ 1/2 teaspoon ground cinnamon
- ◊ 1/2 teaspoon ground nutmeg
- ◊ 1/2 teaspoon bicarbonate of soda
- ◊ lemon juice to taste
- ◊ chopped coriander to taste
- ◊ salt and black pepper to taste

METHOD

Sauté the carrot, onion in the butter or ghee. Add the bicarbonate of soda.

Keep sautéing until the onion is transparent.

Add all the spices and sauté until the onion and carrot are brown and smelling sweet.

Add the lentil puree and mix thoroughly until warm.

Remove from heat and add the ingredients to taste.

Serve warm with a decoration of coriander leaves or flat-leaved parsley.

GARNISHING AND SERVING IDEAS
FOR BEAN DIPS

As you've seen from the preceding pages bean dips encompass a wide range of flavors and themes, nevertheless there are some general approaches we can take.

The Middle-Eastern type dips, like hummus, or dips made from a white bean, are best garnished with a dry, ground spice and a complementary finishing oil. A mild-flavored spice with a strong color like sweet paprika is ideal however you can also use something like sumac or turmeric, just use a lighter touch. Your finishing oil should complement, rather than over-power the dip, which is why olive oil is the classic favorite, however, other oils like avocado and macadamia are deliciously different.

My favorite dippers for the Middle Eastern dips are flat breads, like Lebanese bread, or semi-flat breads, like Turkish bread.

In keeping with the Middle Eastern theme if you can find bowls with geometric designs the effect is dramatic and also looks great.

The more Mexican-themed bean dips or dips made from darker beans are best garnished with some pretty leaves of parsley or coriander, or some finely sliced pieces of a small, sweet pepper or jalapeno or very thin slices of lime. A dob of sour cream or salsa (or both) on an otherwise dark, plain-looking dip really lifts it up. The classic pairing of Mexican dips (bean based or otherwise) is, of course, the corn chip unflavored. However, there are some who like the combination of a dip with a nacho cheese flavored corn chip and I don't see why you should deny yourself if this is the way your taste buds swing. As with other culture-bound foods if you can find a bowl with a Central American design that would work beautifully.

Miso dips and spreads don't really lend themselves to garnish since the flavors are so particular. They're best paired with rice crackers plain, sesame or seaweed flavored.

For a further Japanese feel I'd suggest serving miso dips on one of those flat, rectangular ceramic plates that you can get from a Japanese-themed store or even on or in lacquerware.

VEGETABLE DIPS AND SPREADS

DELICIOUS AND GOOD FOR YOU TOO

Although vegetables feature heavily in the clear majority of dips, there are some dips whose bulk and base comes from vegetable. Theoretically, you could use any starchy vegetable puree as the base of a dip; carrot, pumpkin and sweet potato come immediately to mind. Other vegetables also lend themselves well to becoming the main focus of a dip think artichoke, broccoli, cauliflower, eggplant and zucchini and, of course, a whole range of salsas made from tomato.

But whatever the vegetable, I have devoted several pages (pages 206 to 216) to the art of caramelization through slow pan-frying or baking. Taking that little bit of extra effort to allow the vegetables to slow-cook in their own juices allows the miracle of the Maillard Reaction to take place and gives a range of depth and complexity that you could never get just by immersing in boiling water.

So, welcome to the world of Vegetable Dips.

Baba Ganoush

a.k.a. Baba Ghanoush a.k.a. Baba Ghannouj …

One of the classic Middle Eastern dips and even though it's another one of those dips that require cooking its deliciousness is well worth the effort.

STORAGE:

Refrigerated for up to four days but must be covered with a thin layer of oil at the top.

Preparation Time: Anything from 45 to 90 minutes, depending on your method.

INGREDIENTS

- ◊ 500 g (1 lb) Charred Eggplant (page 207), skin removed
- ◊ 3 cloves of garlic
- ◊ juice from 1 lemon (more if desired)
- ◊ 60 ml (2 oz) tahini (more if desired)
- ◊ 90 ml (3 oz) extra-virgin olive oil (more if desired for serving)
- ◊ 60 g (2 oz) finely chopped parsley

METHOD

Place lemon juice, garlic, oil and tahini in a food processor and pulse until well blended. Add eggplant and pulse until you have a texture that you like. The classic baba ganoush is always a little rough around the edges since its often hand-made, mashed with a fork and in a stirred in a bowl until it's a thick paste. Feel free to do it like this if you don't want to use a food processor.

Stir in most of the parsley by hand.

Transfer dip to a serving bowl. Use the remaining parley, sprinkled on top and use some extra olive oil to drizzle on the top. Serve at room temperature.

VARIATIONS

If baking the eggplants in the oven, roast some garlic too and use the roast garlic for the dip instead of the fresh garlic. You can also finish with a sprinkle of smoked paprika.

In Israel some substitute mayonnaise for the tahini and call the result Salat Hatzilim.

You can also use charred courgettes or zucchini of the same quantity to make a zucchini baba ganoush, resulting in a very finely flavored dip, subtler than its eggplant cousin.

Quick and Dirty

If you don't want to go to the trouble of charring your own eggplant, you can buy pre-charred eggplant in oil. The best value way to buy them is in those large jars that you can get from specialty Italian delicatessens. Just drain off the excess oil and remove the skins. Then bung them straight into the food processor with the other ingredients (but leave out the olive oil, since store-bought eggplant will already be oily enough). The results aren't half bad. Not dirty at all, really.

A staple of Tunisian cuisine and one of the few dips that require any cooking, harissa is highly versatile and used as a sauce condiment to flavor meat, fish and roasted vegetables but it works equally well as a dip.

STORAGE:

Refrigerated for up to four days but must be covered with a thin layer of oil at the top.

Preparation time: About 30 minutes.

INGREDIENTS

◊ 2 or 3 large red capsicums / bell peppers - about 500 g (1 pound)

◊ 1 teaspoon caraway seeds

◊ 1 teaspoon coriander seeds

◊ 1 teaspoon cumin seeds

◊ 6 cloves of garlic, coarsely chopped

◊ 3 or 4 hot chilis, seeds removed

◊ 2 medium Spanish onion, coarsely chopped - about 170 grams (6 oz)

◊ juice from 2 lemons (more if desired)

◊ 60 ml (2 fl oz) tomato paste (more if desired)

◊ 60 ml (2 fl oz) extra-virgin olive oil (more if desired for serving)

◊ salt to taste

METHOD

First wash the capsicums, halve them and remove the seeds and the thin tissue that connects the seeds to the rest of the flesh.

Cook your capsicums. There are a couple different ways of doing this. Pick your favorite.

Cover a rimmed baking sheet in foil. Take the halved capsicums and place them on the sheet, cut sides down, in a single layer and bake them in the oven until charred on the skin.

If you're feeling super adventurous and you have gas burners, using a pair of tongs char the capsicums directly onto the flame, skin-side down.

Whichever way you do it, the capsicum should be cooked so that it's tender and has lost all its raw crunch.

One cooked, wrap the eggplants in foil and leave to rest for about 15 minutes. This will allow steam from the capsicum to loosen the skin.

Carefully peel off the skin from the capsicum flesh. This should be fairly easy to do if you've cooked the flesh until it's tender and you've left them to rest long enough in the foil. Scoop out the eggplant flesh with a spoon and set aside in a bowl. If there are any charred bits of skin then pick the bits out, or feel free to leave a little bit in if you like the charred flavor.

In a dry fry pan or dry cast iron pan, lightly toast the caraway, coriander, and cumin seeds. This should only take a couple of minutes. You'll know they're ready when you can smell the spices but there's no burnt smell.

Remove the spices and place in a mortar and pestle. Grind to a coarse or fine powder depending on your preference.

Heat the frying pan over a medium heat. Add the oil and quickly fry the garlic and chilies until almost brown due to caramelization. Quickly add the onions and fry until they lose only a little of their color.

Take the capsicum, ground spices, fried garlic, chili and onions and the tomato paste and lemon juice and blitz in a food processor until you have a smooth paste.

Serve with drizzling oil at room temperature.

VARIATIONS

Harissa recipes vary from region to region. Some recipes use long, sweet red chilis instead of capsicum. Others add paprika to the spices. You can also add coarse-chopped parsley or fresh coriander/ground coriander seed to the mixture.

One particularly interesting variation is Rose Harissa. Take three tablespoons of dried rose petals that have been left to soak in boiling water for a few minutes, then drained and pat dried with a paper towel. Then gently blend them in to finished recipe above right at the end. Leave some petals as a garnish. They will impart a subtle and mysterious quality to the dip and certainly a talking point. You can find food-quality rose petals at specialty Middle Eastern delicatessens.

VARIATIONS

Muhammara

This is the Syrian version of harissa. The walnuts and pomegranate molasses give it a special character. Using the recipe above as a base blitz in the following:

◊   60 g (2 oz) breadcrumbs

◊   60 g (2 oz) walnuts

◊   20-45 ml (2/3 - 1 1/2 oz) pomegranate molasses

◊   olive oil to taste

Ajika

The Georgian red pepper dip is traditionally made using boiled red peppers, but you can also use green or any other color and you can grill the peppers instead. What makes this version special is that you start with the harissa recipe above then use, in addition, to taste, walnuts and a mountain herb called blue fenugreek - Utskho Suneli to the natives. Since blue fenugreek doesn't exactly leap off the shelves of supermarkets outside of Caucasia, use ordinary fenugreek instead.

Artichoke Dip

This is a super-rich dip that's definitely to be taken in small quantities, but since most humans are hard-wired

to love fat and salt it's unlikely that people are going to be dainty about it so it's best to prepare this in 'Party Size' amounts.

INGREDIENTS

◊ 2 cans (about 750g or 1.5 lb) of canned artichokes, thoroughly drained

◊ 210 g (8 oz) of parmesan cheese

◊ 100 g (4 oz) of sour cream

◊ 1 medium sized Caramelized Onion (page 215), medium diced

Finely sliced scallion, spring onion or chives for decoration.

METHOD

Pre-heat oven to 200°C (400°F).

Blitz cheese and cream until smooth.

Add artichokes and onion and blitz in pulses until mixed in, but not chopped up too finely. You want this dip to be slightly lumpy.

Bake for about 20 minutes in a ceramic baking dish or in one of those country-style terracotta baking dishes (if you have one) until there's a slight brown crust on top.

Decorate and serve warm, preferably in the same dish you baked it in.

NOTES:

Some similar recipes call for the addition of mayonnaise to thin this very rich dip, but they ask that the mayonnaise be added before baking. This is crazy because heat destroys mayonnaise and forces it to split, turning it basically into oil with a bit of egg in it. So, I never take a recipe that calls for cooking mayonnaise seriously. If you find this dip needs a little thinning add the mayonnaise after cooking, when the dip is warm, not hot, to minimize the splitting.

VARIATIONS

You can use cream cheese instead of the sour cream

To make Warm Spinach and Artichoke Dip you can replace half the quantity of artichoke and replace it with 375 g (3/4 lb) of frozen spinach that's been thawed and drained.

You can forget the artichoke altogether and have a Warm Spinach and Green Pepper Dip. Just use 375 g (3/4 lb) each of drained, thawed frozen spinach and the same quantity of green capsicum (green bell pepper) that's been grilled or baked (page 210) and then medium diced. Remember not to blitz the vegetable too much in this dip. Its charm is in its lumpiness.

Other additions include

A small amount of Caramelized Mushrooms (page 214)

A small amount of fried bacon, chopped into small pieces.

Sweet Potato, Pumpkin and Potato Dips

As far as texture is concerned, and even to the extent of flavor, sweet potato and pumpkin are compatible, substitutable and mixable so a recipe that calls for one can use the other, or a mixture of the two as well.

Potato is a rather bland cousin, unless you get one of those incredibly nice, buttery potato varieties that bake beautifully in the jacket and from which you can get a more flavorsome mash.

To about 400 g (14 oz) of puree made by blitzing the appropriate amount of mashed potato, Caramelized Sweet Potato or Pumpkin (page 213) or even a mixture of any two or all three you can make:

Miso, Sesame and Sweet Potato or Pumpkin Dip

ADD AND BLITZ:

◊   2 tablespoons of tahini

◊   2 tablespoons of miso

◊   a splash of soy sauce

◊   Toasted Sesame Seeds (page 218), to garnish

Sweet Potato / Pumpkin and Cashew Hummus

ADD AND BLITZ:

◊ 1 can of drained, rinsed chickpeas

◊ 4 cloves of Caramelized Garlic (page 210)

◊ a small handful of Roasted Cashews (page 218) chopped finely. If not roasting your own cashews it's harder to find unsalted roasted cashews, so give your cashews a rinse, then pat dry with a paper towel before chopping.

◊ 20 ml (2/3 fl oz) of maple syrup OR two teaspoons of honey

◊ 1 teaspoon of smoked paprika

◊ 1 teaspoon of cumin

◊ 45 ml (1 1/2 fl oz) Greek yoghurt, Labneh (page 66), mayonnaise or sour cream depending on your preference (optional)

◊ A good squeeze of lemon juice (optional)

Skordalia

I couldn't have a dip book without mentioning Skordalia, a classic Greek potato dip.

INGREDIENTS

◊ 500 g (1 lb) of potato mash, preferably still warm.

◊ a whole bulb of garlic that's about 10 cloves. I'm not kidding. With Skordalia, it's ALL about the garlic.

◊ 210 ml (7 fl oz) of olive oil

◊ About 60 ml of white or white wine vinegar.

◊ Salt to taste

METHOD

Blitz the combined ingredients until they're thoroughly mixed into a smooth paste suitable for dipping.

If the mixture is too thick, add more water, oil or vinegar to your taste.

Serve chilled or at room temperature.

NOTES:

You might want to thoroughly mush up the garlic before adding it to the rest of the ingredients to get a better mixture.

Traditionally skordalia is as white as possible, but if you're using a baked potato mash and caramelized garlic you'll end up with an unusual yellowish skordalia that's best served warm.

I think that lemon juice is a perfectly acceptable alternative to white or white wine vinegar.

If you reduce the amount of garlic to two cloves and add about 200 g (7 oz) of tarama or salted fish roe (either yellow or red), you have a nice gluten free taramasalata.

(for the Bread-Based Taramasalata, see page 92).

Another Touch of Mexico

Guacamole, Esquites and Salsa

The following three dips continue the Mexican theme we first explored with the bean dips in the previous section. The true origins of guacamole, esquites and salsa might be lost to time, but they are now firmly placed in our minds as Mexican. Make these three dips up at once, grab a bag of corn chips, sit yourself under a sunlamp while listening to Mariachi music in view of a potted cactus, and it'll be almost like being there - especially if enough tequila or mezcal is involved.

Guacamole

The name comes from the Aztec word for avocado salad. It's so simple to make, I'm not even going to bother writing out the recipe properly.

Just mash three large avocadoes with a fork in a bowl. Squeeze in some lemon or lime juice to taste. Bit of salt. Bit of black pepper. Maybe, at a pinch, some mayonnaise (even though the Aztecs didn't have mayonnaise) or maybe some olive oil (even though the Aztecs didn't have olives). It doesn't have to be smooth as silk. I actually like a guacamole that's a little lumpy, it feels more real, but the result you get from your mushing depends on the type of avocado you get and at what time of the year you acquire it. You might have to resort to a stick blender. Finally add one tomato from which you've removed the seeds and pulp and then medium diced. Fold the tomato in so that it doesn't mush up too much. Serve cold. If you like a touch of heat, add some chili of your choice, either a powder or a dash of hot sauce. That's it.

If you want you can make guacamole in a mortar and pestle. Even if you don't make it in a mortar and pestle you can serve it in one to give people the impression that you have. Then you can make up some story about how making it this way really put you in touch with the food. Half of cooking is theatre.

Esquites Dip

Esquites is a corn salad, served in a small bowl, but a little blitzing turns it into a nice corn dip.

INGREDIENTS

◊ 500 g (1 lb) corn kernels either thawed frozen (my preference) or cut off about 5 or 6 corn cobs.

◊ 4 tablespoons of Cotija cheese (substitute grated Parmesan if unavailable)

◊ juice from 1 or 2 limes

◊ 2 cloves of crushed garlic

◊ 1 jalapeno pepper, de-seeded and finely chopped

◊ 10 g (1/3 oz) tablespoons of finely chopped coriander (cilantro)

◊ 1-2 tablespoons of Crema Mexicana (use mayonnaise if unavailable)

◊ salt, pepper and dried chili flakes to taste

◊ oil for frying (corn oil if you want to stay authentic)

METHOD

Make sure that your frying pan preferably a cast iron one is superhot. Sauté the corn until it starts popping a bit and the kernels get little bits of brown on them. 'Sauté' literally means 'jumped' so you're going to have to make the stuff you're frying jump. Unless you have a very large pan you're going to have to do this step in several batches. Keep a lid on things unless you plan to find mummifying corn kernels over the next six months in your kitchen in places where they've jumped.

Now put the popped, brown kernels in a bowl with all the other ingredients and blend them all together.

Take half the mixture out and blitz until creamy, then mix the creamed mixture with the half you didn't blitz and blend together for a sticky lump of deliciousness that goes really well with the guacamole and the salsa. Serve cold.

NOTES:

Like so many traditional foods the recipe for esquites depends on who you talk to. Some people don't pop the corn and that's completely OK. I like to add thin slices of cucumber and radish. You don't have to blitz this mixture, you can add it to guacamole to fill it out and make an interesting hybrid guacamole esquites with makes for a very satisfying dip.

The real esquites also contains a few finely sliced leaves of a herb called epazote. Epazote can be hard to find outside Mexico, but can't be substituted because this is one of those times a particular flavor is irreplaceable. If you're lucky enough to have a specialty Central American or South American grocery store to hand then see if you can pick up some of the dried stuff. But use it very cautiously, it's very strong and rather special and not to everyone's liking.

Salsa

Although the word 'Salsa' literally just means 'sauce' it's come to mean the fresh cold dips that are associated with Mexican food.

Here's the classic tomato salsa recipe that you can build on Pico de Gallo. Literally it means 'Rooster Pickings', but don't let that put you off.

Pico de Gallo

INGREDIENTS

◊ 6 tomatoes - seeded and medium diced. Cherry tomatoes also work, but you'll need enough to make about 300 g (10 oz)

◊ 1/2 red or Spanish onion finely diced

◊ 1/2 jalapeno - seeded and finely diced

◊ large handful fresh coriander, parsley or mint chopped

◊ 1 or 2 cloves of fresh garlic minced

◊ juice of 1/2 to 1 lime

◊ pinch of ground cumin, salt and black pepper to taste

METHOD

Combine the ingredients in a bowl and stir until well mixed.

Refrigerate for several hours and serve cold.

NOTES:

The basic flavor profile of salsa is the lime, garlic and jalapeno. Coriander is nice too, but a lot of people don't like it, which is why parsley or mint will do at a pinch. Some people like to add a little olive oil too. Given the classic Pico de Gallo base, you can add to the tomato, or replace it with medium dices of the following:

◊ avocado

◊ mango

◊ peach

- ◊ paw paw or papaya
- ◊ pineapple
- ◊ watermelon

SOME LIKE TO ADD A LITTLE HOT SPICE. TYPICALLY:

- ◊ cayenne
- ◊ chili

Now some might argue that this salsa is a little too chunky to be a dip. However, there's nothing stopping you from giving it a few blitz pulses with a stick blender and stirring until you get a texture that you like. You can go right up to a smooth paste, although I wouldn't recommend it. Salsa should always be a little chunky. However *never* do this if you're using watermelon. Watermelon is much too fragile and will liquify much too easily. You're making dip, not some Mexican watermelon gazpacho.

Beetroot and Carrot Dips

Even people who aren't all that crazy about beetroots in general can enjoy a beetroot dip though some are plainly fanatical about them. The deep reddish-purple color is certainly spectacular and beetroot dips go well as an accompanying dip especially with hummus and labneh. Now you can be a purist and bake your beetroots in the same way that you do Caramelized Sweet Potato (page 213), but really, most of us just use the canned stuff.

The texture of baked carrot is much the same as for beetroot and so as far as the method of making goes, the two root vegetables are interchangeable. The flavor, of course, is different but the same herbs and spices work for both, so they have complimentary flavor profiles. Of course, with carrot you get a lovely orange color instead of beetroot's red-purple. In fact, two dips, one of each type look quite spectacular next to each other on the table so why not make up a batch of each and impress your friends.

METHOD

For once I'm going to give you the method first because it's always the same method. beetroot and carrot dips are all easy to prepare because you just blitz all the ingredients together to your hearts content.

Just make sure that:

◊ The beetroot, if you're using canned beetroot, is well drained or the resulting dip will be too mushy.

◊ The carrots are well-cooked or they won't mush up enough to make a dip with the right texture.

All beetroot/carrot dips should be served chilled after at least an hour in the refrigerator to allow the flavors to blend.

So, for the recipes below, just think 'carrot' if you're using carrot instead of beetroot.

Classic Beetroot Dip

◊ 500 g beetroot. Baby beet works best, I think, and chop them up a little to make them easier to blitz.

◊ 2 garlic cloves

◊ juice of 1/2 to 1 lemon

◊ 1 teaspoon each of:

◊ ground cinnamon

◊ ground coriander seeds

◊ ground cumin

◊ sweet paprika

◊ olive oil to taste

◊ salt and pepper to taste

NOTES:

Feel free to dry roast the coriander and cumin seeds in a frypan or cast-iron pan for a minute to release their flavors.

You can add labneh or Greek-style yoghurt to any of these dips, but this change does alter the character, color and the vegan status of the dip, but that's entirely a matter of your personal preference.

VARIATIONS

BELL PEPPER / CAPSICUM BEETROOT DIP

To the classic dip add 1 or 2 large slices of charred red or yellow bell pepper either made yourself (page 210) or out of a jar. If out of a jar, drain the oil thoroughly. Although this works with both beetroot and carrot I think that the carrot version works better.

LABNEH BEETROOT DIP

Add 240 ml (8 fl oz) of Labneh (page 66) or Greek-style yoghurt to the classic dip

Turkish Beetroot/Carrot Dip

For this dip you'll have to bake your beetroot (page 213) until you have 400 g (14 oz) and then all you add is the labneh or Greek-style yoghurt, a clove or two of garlic and olive oil to taste. In Turkey the beetroot version is called Kiz Guzeli and the carrot version is called Yoghurtlu Havuc.

DUKKHA BEETROOT DIP

To the classic dip add 50 g of Dry Roasted Hazelnuts and 50 Grams of Dry Roasted Sesame Seeds (page 218). Grind these up first and then blitz them in to the rest of the ingredients.

You can add a little labneh or Greek-style yoghurt to this too.

SESAME BEETROOT

For a bit more of a sesame kick add 4 teaspoons of tahini to the Classic Dip.

MOROCCAN BEETROOT

For even more of a Middle Eastern feel add 45 ml (1 1/2 fl oz) of harissa (page 141) and 4 teaspoons of tahini. If you're using carrot, I recommend also adding 4 teaspoons of ground turmeric or turmeric paste. This will really lift the color.

SUNFLOWER BEETROOT

Add 60 g (2 oz) of Blitzed Toasted Sunflower Seeds (page 218) and serve with 15 g (1/2 oz) of chopped fresh coriander or Italian parsley roughly mixed in.

UMAMI BEETROOT OR CARROT

To add an interesting further layer of flavor, but maintaining a vegan feel, I suggest adding anything from a teaspoon to a tablespoon of vegan vegetable stock powder. I'm inclined to think that this works better with carrot dip than with beetroot dip, but that's up to you to determine. You can also try a bit of miso (page 114). Regardless of whether you're using stock powder or miso, I wouldn't add any more salt, as both these additives are salty enough as they are.

Storage Note:

All these dips freeze well and will keep for months in the freezer. However, if you intend to make them in advance for freezing I recommend that you don't mix in the leafy greens like coriander or parsley. Just leave them out of the recipes altogether and just put them in once you've thawed out the dips and are ready to serve them.

Tapenade

Ahhhhh, tapenade. Where would olive lovers be without the occasional hit of tapenade? Tapenade originated in the Provencal region of France, but as I said in the introduction (for those of you who could be bothered reading introductions), tapenade or dips like it are probably as old as olive cultivation itself. Expensive to buy but cheap to make at home, this dip/spread is worth your time to find just the right blend that appeals to you.

But, as usual, it all starts with the basics:

INGREDIENTS

◊ 500 g (1 lb) of olives, pitted and drained of the oil or brine they've been bathing in

◊ 1 tablespoon of capers, drained of the brine that they've been bathing in

◊ 2 cloves of garlic, minced

◊ 1 or 2 anchovies (optional)

METHOD

Blitz all the ingredients with short pulses until you get a texture that's still lumpy, but has enough smoothness to stick together. Serve cold.

You can also mush everything up in a mortar and pestle.

You can also simple finely chop everything together if you want to be traditional and artisany about it.

NOTES:

Traditionally tapenade is made with black olives, such as black Spanish olives, but there's no reason that you can't use green olives or any other variety. If you're going to use green olives it's probably best not to use ones with pimentos or any other fillings. Kalamata makes for a rather rich tapenade but might be a little too salty for some tastes.

Also traditional is the addition of anchovy. Err on the light touch with those little fish as they can easily overwhelm the olive.

Olivarum Conditurae a.k.a Epityrum

Here is the recipe for one of the most ancient dips for which we have any written records, courtesy of Mr Lucius Junius Moderatus Columella (4 CE 70 CE). Originally epityrum was a Greek dip then the Romans did what Romans did with nearly all things Greek and appropriated it for their own purposes.

INGREDIENTS

◊ 210 g (7 oz) green olives, pitted and finely diced

◊ 1 leek, finely sliced

◊ 2 or 3 sticks of celery, finely sliced

◊ 4 or 5 leaves of common mint

◊ 4 or 5 leaves of rue or fenugreek, finely sliced

◊ 20 ml (2/3 fl oz) vinegar or mead

◊ 1 teaspoon of honey

◊ 60 ml (2 oz) olive oil for frying plus extra if necessary for dressing

METHOD

Sauté the leek in the olive oil until limp. If you don't like your garlic on the raw side you can sauté it at the same time as the leek, or use Caramelized Garlic (page 210).

Remove from leek from heat and put it on a cutting board with the other ingredients.

Using a large knife chop the leek up and mix it in with the other ingredients. The Romans didn't have food processors.

Serve chilled. Feel free to add more oil if you like.

NOTES:

Both rue and fenugreek leaves are very strongly flavored so I recommend a light touch as you might not like the results. Ancient Roman gourmands were used to much stronger flavors than we are.

If you can get your hands on it, apple mint works well with this, particularly if you're going to use mead instead of vinegar.

Veering further away from tradition you could use chopped, drained artichoke hearts instead of celery.

An even earlier variation of Epityrum quoted in his book De Agricultura (On Agricultural Matters) by Cato the Elder (234 BCE 149 BCE) adds a pinch each of ground coriander, ground cumin and fennel and foregoes the celery and garlic altogether. In fact, Cato's recipe only says 'Fennel'. If you use chopped up fennel bulb, you'll get something similar to Olivarum Conditurae but with an aniseedy twist. If you use fennel seed you'll get something closer to our modern idea of tapenade but with an aniseedy twist. Either way, both options are delicious.

PESTO

I'll be frank with you, I don't consider pesto to be a dip so much as an amazing sauce. Real pesto is much too strong a flavor for dipping on its own, and I think it's much better used as an additional flavoring or finishing to a more neutral dip (pesto hummus, anyone?) or for the original purpose for which it was intended to make spaghetti or fettucine marvellous. Nevertheless, you'll find pesto as a dip in the supermarket, so I think that there'll be complaints if I don't include pesto here. Fortunately, it's super easy.

INGREDIENTS

◊ 100 g (3 1/2 oz approximately) of fresh basil leaves. Leaves only, don't use the stems.

◊ 100 g (3 1/2 oz approximately) of grated parmesan or Romano cheese

◊ 100 g (3 1/2 oz approximately) of chopped pine nuts or walnuts

◊ 100 ml (3 1/2 oz approximately) of extra virgin olive oil

◊ 2 to 4 cloves of garlic

◊ 1 teaspoon of oregano leaves or to taste (optional)

◊ pepper to taste (It's already got enough salt from the cheese)

METHOD

Throw everything in a processor or in a bowl and use a stick blender and blitz.

Refrigerate until needed, with a layer of oil on top it will keep for months and just get better and better as time goes on.

NOTES:

I keep saying 'approximately' for the amounts of the ingredients because equal quantities of the main ingredients are just your starting points. This pesto is a little thick because it's going to be a dip or a spread. I'd add more oil if I were going to make it suitable as a pasta sauce.

Lots of people use pine nuts in a pesto, but my mother taught me to make it with walnuts and I really like the robustness that walnuts impart. I also like to keep some of the walnuts out of the processing and just chop them roughly and add them later to give the pesto a more country-style roughness. I do the same country roughness thing by reserving a little of the basil too.

I also like a peppery and garlicky pesto, so I'll add lots of pepper and enough garlic to bring tears to your eyes. See my Cures for Garlic Breath (page 212), you'll need them if you choose to go down this path. This is one time when I think you need the raw garlic for the oomph although if you're not a garlic fan give the Caramelized Garlic (page 210) a try.

The World's Easiest Dip

Oregano Garlic Tomato

Finally, the world's easiest dip, and it's yummy.

Take a bunch of tomatoes and slice them about a small finger width through their cross-sections into discs.

Place them in single layer in a wide, shallow plate or on a cookie baking tray.

Sprinkle a couple of cloves of drushed fresh garlic evenly over them.

Sprinkle about 4 teaspoons of oregano evenly over them.

Sprinkle a little salt and black pepper.

Now leave this in the refrigerator for several hours so that the tomatoes go all limp and the oregano calms down a little.

Once the tomatoes are noticeably mushier put the whole lot into a bowl and roughly chop them with a knife or

fork - whatever works for you. This dip should always be a little rough. Or, if you like it really rough you can dip and eat straight from the preparation dish, which is what we always used to do.

It works best with a white crusty bread like a baguette, although super-fresh Lebanese bread works fine too.

Enjoy and thank my mother for this one, while you're at it.

GARNISHING AND SERVING IDEAS FOR VEGETABLE DIPS

Of all the dips and spreads, the vegetable dips offer the widest variety in terms of texture and color. They look fine on their own and for the most part need no more garnishing than a sprig of coriander, parsley or even mint.

So getting the best presentation out of a vegetable dip is more about the color and texture of the serving bowl.

Now there's nothing wrong with being subtle and simply putting everything in white bowls, or clear glass or earthenware. But if you're thinking party, as in an informal, kick your heels up party (as opposed to sit down, haute-cuisine party with a chamber orchestra playing in the background) then you'd might as well go dramatic. This is where basic color theory is your best friend.

The most dramatic effects come from pairing colors from opposite sides of the color wheel, so your best bets for dramatic are:

Yellow dips blue bowls	Green dips red bowls
Red dips green bowls	Orange dips purple bowls
Brown dips white bowls	White dips black bowls

Be playful.

SWEET STUFF AND NUT BUTTERS

Amazingly, the same base dip that works so well with seafood dips works really well with sweet dips. This should come as no surprise to those who have ever made cheesecake or who have blended whipped sour cream with a hint of lime marmalade to create an amazing accompaniment to a flourless orange cake.

Making sweet dips is super simple, you just add a small amount of fruit puree or conserve or jam to your base of cream cheese with sour cream, mascarpone, crème fraiche, Greek-style yoghurt or labneh, or in addition, ricotta (but not mayonnaise, obviously). To this you can also add a sweet spice such as a touch of nutmeg or the merest hint of clove. A dusting of ground cinnamon is as effective on a bowl of sweet dip as a dusting of paprika on hummus.

And if you want something that's more a spread than a dip, just have more cream cheese in your mixture than labneh, yoghurt or crème fraiche.

If you have a sweet tooth, I suggest adding icing sugar to your base before you add any additional fruit.

As I said, it's easy. However, there are some things that you should consider.

The 'drier' fruits, such as banana, figs, berries, or even pineapples, work. The wetter ones like orange or grapes, won't.

However, you can make a pretty effective puree by blitzing sultanas or raisins that have been soaking a little in water, or, if you're entertaining adults, a fortified wine like sherry or port (white port in particular) or a fruit-flavored alcohol like Cointreau (then you can have your oranges!)

If using fresh fruit, you're better off using it as decoration and make a puree from frozen fruit.

When frozen fruit, especially frozen berries, thaw out, they leave a lot of juice. Rescue this juice, throw it in a saucepan with a little icing sugar, get it to reduce a little until it's noticeably thicker, then pour this reduced, sweetened juice into a serving bowl, wait for it to cool a little, then mix in the sweetened dip base.

You can think of any jam, marmalade or conserve as a sort of puree waiting for your sweetened base to make a dip. Explore and experiment. You might even finally be able to use that ginger and plum jam that your Aunt Mabel gave you eight Christmases ago and that you've never used. It'll still be good. It'll probably still be edible when archaeologists dig it up hundreds of years from now if you decide not to open it after all.

Feel free to experiment with chocolate too. Mix enough chocolate powder and icing sugar into your base dip and you'll end up with something that tastes a lot like chocolate cheesecake.

What do you do with a sweet dip?

In most cases, you'll use it like a spread, on bread or toast. However, more thinly textured sweet dips work well with wedges of apple, with sweet biscuits, like almond biscotti or crostoli or as a more unorthodox dip for churros or a more unorthodox filling for brandy snaps or cannoli.

SEED AND NUT BUTTERS · THE BASICS

Nuts are actually seeds, so the distinction between the two is more a culinary one than a real, botanic one. What distinguishes the seeds that are suitable for spreads as opposed to other seeds that humans consume such as grains (wheat, rye, barley), pseudo-grains (buckwheat, millet, quinoa) and legumes (beans, peas, lentils) is their oil content. It's the oil in the seeds and nuts that, when released from the cells through grinding or processing, that gives us the non-dairy 'butters' that are suitable for spreads. *With a little imagination and a sense of playfulness you can have quite a bit of fun with nut butters.*

MAKING SEED AND NUT BUTTERS

Yes, you can spend hundreds of dollars and buy specialty machines that make nut butters and it's worth the investment if you're making commercial quantities or if you're a super nut butter fan, but you can get very reasonable results using a food processor. Unfortunately, experiments in making nut butters with blenders haven't yielded very good results, because blender motors aren't powerful enough to handle the rigours of nut butters. So, unless you're interested in using a mortar and pestle and hand-grinding your seeds and nuts and developing very powerful forearms in the process the food processor is the way to go.

The basic technique is the same for all the butters.

NOTE:

As with roasting, different nuts behave in different ways so only make ONE type of nut butter at a time. If you want to blend the nuts blend the finished butters together.

Start with about 50 ml (1 2/3 oz) of a thick, nuetral oil, like grapeseed, sunflower, safflower or canola, and put it into a food processor. This should be enough for about 500 g (1 pound) of seeds or nuts.

If you have the same oil as the seed or nut that you're using, that's ideal, but otherwise a low-flavor oil like coconut oil or palm oil is just fine. The advantage of coconut or palm oil is that they stay relatively solid at room temperature and help to provide a buttery texture. A liquid oil tends to thin out the butter too much. This oil is just to get the process going. As you add the seeds and nuts the seed or nuts own oils will start to get released and continue the process on its own.

Add the nuts gradually. The mixture will go through various stages:

Initially the nuts will turn into granules

Then into a powder

Then the powder will clump and ball

Eventually the mixture turns into a paste.

Take care not to burn your food processor motor. If the processor has been running for longer than four minutes then turn it off and let it cool down for about five minutes before continuing.

The consistency of the butter will depend on its temperature and the oil content. It's natural that while it's in the processor the butter will be more fluid because its warmer but as it cools to room temperature it will return to a pastier consistency. So only ever add more oil if the processor has been going for a while and you feel that the flour isn't turning into a paste. Always add only a little oil, no more than a teaspoon, at a time.

If you've added too much oil don't panic. Oil tends to naturally separate from the nut butter and you can always pour some off and keep it as a finishing oil or as a cooking oil for other purposes. You can also add more oil later if you like.

NOTES:

Once you've achieved a consistency that you like, you can decide if you want to add salt to your seed or nut butter to your taste.

If you want to make a 'crunchy butter' then simply grind up a small quantity of nuts beforehand and add them to the smooth butter right at the end.

Sweetening

If you're going to go down on the sweet side make this decision before you make your butter, in order to get a better blend. Liquid sweeteners are best, and the best sweetener for seed and nut butters is honey because it produces a more even result and helps give the nut butter a creamier texture.

Start the sweet nut butter process by using only 30 ml (1 oz) of coconut oil and adding 30 ml (1 oz) of honey.

Pick a mildly flavored honey such as:

◊ blended honey

◊ alfalfa

◊ clover

- ◊ orange blossom
- ◊ yellow box.

A strongly flavored like blueberry, chestnut, buckwheat or the highly unusual leatherwood, can easily overwhelm the seed or nut flavors. That's no reason not to use these honeys, just mix them with a more mildly flavored one.

OTHER SWEETENERS THAT YOU COULD TRY INCLUDE:

- ◊ agave syrup
- ◊ cane syrup
- ◊ maple syrup
- ◊ rose water
- ◊ orange blossom water.

As I said, there's no rule that says that you can only use one type of honey or just one type of other sweetener at a time in the same recipe. Feel free to experiment and find a flavor and texture that works for you.

Spicing Things Up

There are a lot of spices that go well with nut butters, and, since the increasing popularity of previously unusual flavor combinations as salted caramel and chili chocolate it would seem that you could try almost anything.

But if you're just starting out with baby steps, you're safest with the sweet spices such as:

- ◊ allspice
- ◊ cardamom
- ◊ cinnamon
- ◊ cloves

◊ coriander

◊ ginger

◊ mace

◊ nutmeg

… but you're also free to add other flavorings such as …

◊ cranberries

◊ currants

◊ raisins

◊ dark chocolate

◊ cocoa nibs

◊ desiccated or shredded coconut either raw or toasted

◊ vanilla either as an extract or the vanilla bean itself.

A NOTE ON STORAGE:

I've had seed and nut butters that store for months in the refrigerator. Just make sure that if you're going to use your butter, it's best to let it warm up a little to improve spreadability.

SEED AND NUT BUTTER RECIPES AND OTHER FLAVOR PAIRINGS THAT WORK

ALMOND BUTTERS

Almond butters can be made from raw or roasted almonds, blanched and un-blanched. Because almonds have such a mild quality (especially when blanched and raw) they lend themselves to a wide variety of flavor combinations, making the almond the most versatile nuts for spreads.

COCONUT ALMOND BUTTER

Add 60 (2 oz) g of desiccated coconut. This works better with roasted almond than raw almond. But for an added flavor dimension, pan toast the coconut until it browns just slightly.

SWEET SPICE VANILLA ALMOND SPREAD

Add a teaspoon (or more to taste) of vanilla extract to 500 g (1 pound) of almond butter.

The sweet spice can be any combination of the spices I mentioned above, in a quantity that appeals to you. If you use all of them you end up with a Chai Vanilla Almond Butter.

Remember that it takes time for these spices to release their essential oils, so it's better to add small quantities of spice to the butter and then give it a day in the refrigerator to let the flavors mature before attempting any more flavor adjustments.

ALMOND MISO SPREAD

To make this savoury spread add 100 g (3 oz) of Brown or Brown Rice Miso Paste to 400 g (14 oz) of butter made from roasted almonds.

PEPITA ALMOND SPREAD

To make this savoury spread add 100 g (3 oz) of Roasted Pepita or Pumpkin Seed Butter (see page 218) to 400 g (14 oz) of butter made from roasted almonds. Add a teaspoon of garam masala and an optional pinch of chili or Cayenne pepper.

BRAZIL NUT

Brazil nut has a strength of flavor that sneaks up on you, so it's a little too strong on its own, but works well blended with the more softly flavored nuts like almond and cashew.

CASHEW

Because of its high oil content and relatively soft cell walls the cashew lends itself to making the smoothest and silkiest of nut butters. Its medium-strong flavor combines well with either sweet or savoury flavors. Cashew, vanilla and maple syrup works well, as does salted cashew honey.

HAZELNUT

Pure hazelnut butter is so strongly flavored that it's best used blended in combination with a more neutral nut such as almond or peanut (I think it overwhelms cashew, but maybe that's just me). However, a particularly famous commercial spread, Nutella, while not exactly a nut butter, is based on hazelnut and chocolate and in those cases when you can't get your hands on some you can make something that's approximately like it at home.

HAZELNUT CHOCOLATE SPREAD

There are a lot of recipes out there for a spread like this in the big wide world outside of this book, but, frankly, a lot of them don't taste very good. I'm going to give you a recipe that is delicious. The bad news is that it's not exactly 'healthy'. The good news is that it's so rich that you don't need to slather it on in order to enjoy it, so it's relatively healthier as a relatively thin smearing will do.

The best news of all is that I'm going to make this as easy as possible for you.

INGREDIENTS

◊ 200 g (7 oz) of the chocolate of your choice crumbled or chopped up into little pieces and at room temperature

◊ 200 ml (7 oz) cream, with more spare to adjust thickness

◊ 100 g (3 oz) hazelnut flour with more to spare to adjust thickness

◊ vanilla essence to taste

◊ ground cinnamon to taste

METHOD

Put the chocolate, vanilla and cinnamon into a bowl that can take some heat.

Heat the cream in a saucepan until it's just simmering.

Pour the cream into the chocolate bowl and begin stirring until the chocolate is all dissolved.

Pour in the hazelnut flour and keep stirring until thoroughly incorporated.

Store in refrigerator in a jar. It will keep for months but it never lasts that long.

NOTES:

What you have made here, in effect, is a thin ganache, the sort of thing that you decorate cakes with, but thickened with hazelnut to make it more of a spread.

Your results will vary depending on the chocolate that you use. If the mixture is too thick, add some more cream while the mixture is still runny. If it's too thin, add some more hazelnut flour.

If you make this with dark chocolate (which I strongly recommend) you might have to sweeten the mixture with honey or sugar.

If you make this with milk chocolate I might have to disown you, but it will be more appealing to most children, so for this I'll forgive you.

To make a vegan version use a vegan chocolate, substitute the cream for soy milk, preferably one of the thicker brands, and if you need a sweetener, use rice malt.

The great thing about this recipe is that you're not fooling around with double-boilers to melt the chocolate, and if you're mixing it directly in the container in which you'll be storing it in, there's minimal washing up.

Remember that because this spread has NO preservatives, other than the naturally occurring ones in the ingredients, it needs to live in the refrigerator. Because it's going to be cold, you should err to keep it on the firm side, because when it quickly reaches room temperature on the bread it'll go soft and scrumptious.

If you're going to keep it on the thinner side, it makes a totally decadent dip for strawberries, peach slices, apple slices you name it.

MACADAMIA

Macadamia makes an utterly delicious nut butter. Additives should only be used in very small quantities so as not to detract from the delicacy of the flavor. The major disadvantage is price. This is an expensive nut, but almost worth taking out an extension on your mortgage for. Candlenut is similar enough to make it worth experimenting with because it's much cheaper but its bitterness might put many off even when balanced by a sweetener.

PEANUT

Follow the same technique for making peanut butter as for any other nut butter but use peanut oil to help the process along. Whether you get crunchy or smooth will depend on whether or not you reserve some crushed peanut for the final mixing.

Sometimes the only peanuts you'll be able to get are roasted salted. If this is so, this will be way too much salt you'll need to wash the salt off quickly by putting the peanuts in a colander and quickly rinsing under a running tap of cold water. It'll only take a few seconds. Then shake the excess water out and use the peanuts immediately unless you can dry them on a tray in the sun or quickly in the oven for later use.

Most commercial peanut butter is made from roasted peanut. Here's your opportunity to try making it with raw peanut. Raw peanut butter is very different in character to its better-known roasted cousin and has its fans. You can also blend the two types together and see if this works for you too. Making peanut butter at home also lets you control how much sugar you consume, since your home-made butter won't contain any sugar that you haven't put into it yourself.

PECAN

Pecan is a wonderful nut for a nut butter and it works well sweetened with maple syrup. Add a little cinnamon and you essentially get the nut butter equivalent of pecan pie.

PISTACHIO

Makes an amazingly rich nut butter that's delicious on its own but works well with almond and cashew. Like peanut, you can often only get the salted variety so it has to be shelled and rinsed, then dried on a baking tray in the oven before you can use them to make the nut butter. Warda Fustuq is literally just the Arabic for rose pistachio. Add a few drops of rosewater to a honey-sweetened butter made from roasted, unsalted pistachio and you'll end up with a quintessential Middle Eastern flavor.

LEMON PISTACHIO BUTTER

Add 45 ml (1 ½ fl oz) of lemon to a butter made from roasted pistachios. Add a little honey if desired.

WALNUT

Walnuts are amazing, but much too strong to use on their own. Like hazelnut, this works best in combination with almond or peanut.

SEED BUTTERS

SUPER PROTEIN SPREAD

This spread, when served on bread, provides a complete profile of all the essential amino acids and is very tasty too. You can make it at a pinch by toasting 210 g (7 oz) each of the seeds, then blending them all together in the food processor at the same time. You probably won't need to add much coconut or palm oil, because pine nuts are quite oily in their own right. Add a little salt to bring out the flavors more.

Otherwise blend equal quantities of the following seed butters:

> Pumpkin seeds/Pepitas
>
> Sunflower seeds
>
> Pine nuts

TAMARI SUNFLOWER

Add 1 teaspoon of tamari (wheat-free soy sauce) to a butter made from roasted sunflower seeds.

The Joys of Tahini

Tahini is basically a paste made of ground sesame seeds. In the Middle East tahini is often used as a spread on its own, but most Westerners find the taste a little strong, and prefer to use tahini as a flavoring component in other preparations.

Tahini is ancient! The oldest recorded mention of sesame is on clay tablets written about 4000 years ago. And although it's most popular in the Middle East, Tahini is used in many East Asian dishes and in Indian cuisine too.

As a health benefit sesame is also one of the highest vegetarian sources of calcium. So, there's a bonus for you. The main varieties of tahini are:

Hulled. This tahini is made from sesame seeds that have had their outer coating taken off. Its color is light and its flavor rather refined.

Unhulled. This tahini is made from sesame seeds where the outer coating of the seed has been retained. Its color is darker; the flavor nuttier and more robust. It's also richer in calcium because it's in the hull that most of the calcium is found.

Roasted and unroasted. Tahini can also be made from sesame that has been roasted, either in the hulled or unhulled state. The taste of the roast variety is smokier, and the fat level is higher than the equivalent raw varieties. However, as with many seeds the process of roasting makes some of the nutrition in the seed more easily digested and assimilated.

Note on Storage

You buy tahini in sealed jars. These jars have a use-by date and some varieties last longer than other. Unless the label says otherwise, once you open your jar it seems prudent to refrigerate the tahini. Note though that cooling tahini makes it go rigid, so if you're planning to use it take it out of the refrigerator in time to let it soften up, or you'll be in for a tough time getting it out of the jar.

Sesame oil tends to separate from tahini quite easily, forming a layer at the top. This is perfectly normal. Just remember to stir the oil in when you're ready to use the tahini.

DIPPERS WET AND DIPPERS DRY

WET DIPPERS - CRUDITÉS

With all this talk about dips, we need to mention dippers. Crudités are the dipper of choice for the health conscious or the gluten intolerant or the paleo-oriented. 'Crudité' simply means 'raw' so the requirements of crudités are simple. They can be any raw vegetable that:

◊ tastes good raw and whose intrinsic flavor compliments or at least doesn't compete with the flavor of the dip;

◊ is the right shape or can be cut into the right shape to dip and can then be conveniently held either in the hand, or at the end of a toothpick - on one of those elegant bamboo skewers or on those dainty and delicate mini-forks.

HERE'S A LIST OF TIME-HONOURED CLASSIC CRUDITÉS INCLUDING SOME THAT YOU MIGHT NOT HAVE THOUGHT OF:

◊ carrot sticks: which you can now get in orange, yellow, red and purple

◊ cucumber sticks with or without the seeds, with or without the skin on (Lebanese cucumbers work best for this)

◊ capsicum/bell pepper sticks: they come in red, green, yellow, orange and, if you can find them, purple

◊ celery sticks

◊ florets of cauliflower (white and violet) or broccoli (green and purple)

◊ radishes: red or purple

◊ disks or sticks of daikon, the giant white radish

◊ snow peas or any other pea variety that lets you eat the pod too

◊ green beans

◊ cherry tomatoes or any of those other mini, multicolored tomatoes. You'll need toothpicks or little forks. And you'll need to cut them in half - it's hard to get a dip to stick to tomato skin.

◊ firm lettuce leaves like cos

◊ radicchio leaves

◊ witloof a.k.a. chicory or Belgian endive leaves

And, of course, if you've got a little toothpick action happening there's any number of different fruits that you can use if you're doing Sweet Dips.

You're not obligated to use the traditional spread either.

Consider:

A selection in individual cups, so that people don't have to worry about their fingers grubbing up anyone else's crudités.

Individual serving cups with the dip and crudités already in them as single-serve appetizers.

This is where crudités have an advantage over the dry dippers they don't get soggy and break up in the dip, so you can do this sort of thing.

Or communal bowls or jars with the dip and crudités already in them. You can also try out other ideas, like this one, which has slivers of grilled chicken breast as the dipper not exactly a crudité, but an option if you're not a vegetarian.

DRY DIPPERS - BREADS, CRISPBREADS, CRACKERS

The ideal dry dipper is very neutrally flavored or has a flavor that doesn't compete with the flavor of the dip. The dip should always be the star. It should also be strong enough not to break apart in the dip, especially if the dip or spread is thick.

HERE'S A LIST OF DRY DIPPERS THAT WORK WELL:

Gluten Free

Potato chips / crisps crinkle cut because they hold the dip and the corrugations in the chip make it stronger. Avoid thin-sliced chips for dipping they're much too fragile unless they are of the slow-cooked variety. Slow-cooked chips/crisps are great for dipping because they have the virtue of being both thin and strong. Avoid flavored chips. Plain salted is what you want but if you're lucky you can get unsalted chips / crisps because so many dips are going to be already salty enough. Most potato chips are also gluten-free.

Vegetable chips sweet potato chips and beetroot chips are becoming more available now too. Again, these work better if they have not additional flavoring other than salt.

Popcorn as long as it's on toothpicks.

Rice crackers. The sesame-flavored or salt and pepper varieties work well with a lot of dips. The seaweed-flavored rice crackers work particularly well with the Miso Dips (page 114).

Not Gluten-Free

Pretzels even though the dip tends to fall out of the holes.

Crusty bread like baguettes or epis. The crust provides the firmness you need for dipping and spreading.

Toast from any bread, as long as the bread is firm enough, cut into little triangles with the crusts on to give them structural support or cut into strips like the 'soldiers' that you use to eat soft boiled eggs as long as the soldiers are slightly dry and firm so that they don't collapse. To firm them up, just put them in the oven on a baking tray for a few minutes.

Breadsticks

Dipping twists sticks that are usually made from puff pastry that you can make yourself quite easily by buying sheets of store-bought puff, cutting it into strips, twisting the strips and then baking them on a baking tray following the baking instructions that you read on the package label.

Lebanese bread wedges that you can have fresh or toasted. You can make the toasted ones easily by cutting up a round of Lebanese bread like a pizza into, say, 16 slices and then baking them in the oven, even a microwave oven, for a few minutes until the wedges go hard. The oven temperature doesn't matter. You'll get the hang of this in no time.

Any number of store-bought crispbreads, as long as you can break them up into convenient sizes for dipping.

Any number of different store-bought biscuits or crackers as long as they're plain or neutrally flavored like water crackers or those delicious flatbread crackers with seeds distributed throughout them.

You can get a lot of amusement mileage from trying out all the different taste and texture combinations of biscuits, chips, crisps, crackers, crispbreads and breads and testing out for yourself how they work with your dips.

A FINAL WORD
ABOUT PRESENTATION

I hope that the photography in this book has inspired you to realize that presentation of dips and spreads isn't entirely limited to just throwing some stuff into any old bowl and hoping for the best.

With a little imagination and a teeny-weeny bit of extra work - even if it's only a touch of garnish and a finishing oil, herbs and spices, and a judicious and tasteful placement of ingredients you can create colorful, even spectacular presentations that will win the admiration of your friends, the jealousy of your rivals and the love of small children and animals.

And just like the photo on this page, you don't even have to be limited to bowls. The creative use of stones, tiles or slabs of slate can show off your dips with considerable flair and originality. Just make sure that you wash those slabs thoroughly first. You never know where those old roof tiles have been.

Have fun with this stuff.

I wish you many hours of satisfying munching.

Warm Regards,

Xy

APPENDIX
COOKING FOR DIPS
AND SPREADS

PREPARING LEGUMES FOR DIPS AND SPREADS

If you're a purist, you can prepare your beans from scratch.

Using the dried ones:

Pick out the damaged or rubbish legumes of choice first, as well as any small stones or twigs that came with the dried beans/peas/lentils when you bought them. This sorting is especially important with lentils as little stones often find their way into the packaging.

Soak your legumes of choice in water overnight.

Pour off the soaking water and add fresh water. The ratio of beans to water should be about 1 to 2, so for every cup of beans you'll need two cups of water.

DO NOT ADD SALT TO THE COOKING WATER.

Keep them on a low simmer them for at least 6 to 8 hours to make them edible. I define 'low simmer' as that point when there's just a fine line of bubbles on the edge of the cooking water and the side of the pot you're cooking in. You'll know that the beans are done when you can squish or crush one easily between thumb and forefinger into a paste. If they're any mushier and falling apart then they won't be useful for dips, but can be salvaged for soups and stews.

Some legumes, like lentils, require MUCH less cooking time. How long depends on variables like the type of legume, the size and the sort of pot you're cooking them in. Taste your legumes too once they've passed the squish test. Properly cooked legumes shouldn't have any 'raw' taste about them.

IMPORTANT NOTE:

It sounds like cooking legumes is time consuming.

It is.

But it isn't.

The time it takes is all passive. You don't have to watch the beans as they soak unless you're one of those people who enjoy watching grass grow or paint dry.

By far the easiest way to cook beans is to forget about pots and stoves altogether. Just put them in a slow cooker on 'low'. A low setting means that you're much less likely to overcook them and you can basically leave them on overnight.

You don't even have to watch the beans as they simmer.

If you have a slow cooker, you can just put the DRAINED beans in it.

Boil up some water in a kettle and pour over enough to cover the beans.

Put the lid on, set the cooker to LOW, set the timer to 8 hours later and everything should be nice.

Obviously, this is only a rough guide because makes and models of slow cookers vary and so do the results. Read the manufacturer's instructions about cooking beans in their slow cookers first, visit their websites, or give them a call. I'm sure they'd love to hear from you. It helps to justify the existence and expense of their customer service lines.

The important point here is that while the beans are cooking or soaking, you can be doing other things, like baking and caramelizing vegetables or, even more radically, doing something else that doesn't have anything to do with cooking at all.

IF YOU CAN'T BE BOTHERED SOAKING, OR YOU'RE IN A HURRY, THERE'S ALWAYS CANNED

The obvious answer to saving the trouble of soaking and boiling is canned legumes. For many people, canned is just as good and the cannery has done a lot of that work for you anyway, since the canning process is all about soaking and boiling the legumes so that they're sterile enough for canned preservation. Heat also contributes to the breakdown of antinutrients like phytic acid and lectins that stop you from absorbing or utilising the goodness in legumes.

And now for some bad news …

The bad news is that some people might be concerned about or be sensitive to additives and preservatives in cans such as Bisphenol A and salt, so read the label on the cans first. If you're OK with the canned stuff then go ahead and use it, otherwise, soak and boil your own. It's even cheaper than using the canned stuff.

The bad news continues in that legumes also contain complex carbohydrates called oligosaccharides which you can't digest, but that your gut bacteria can.

The worst news is that in digesting these oligosaccharides, your gut bacteria produce methane as a by-product, hence the well-known gassy side effects of eating beans.

But there is light at the end of the tunnel. You CAN lessen the gassy side effects …

If you think ahead, there's no law that says that you can't soak even canned legumes in water overnight in the refrigerator to leach out any of those undigestible carbs. Remember, after soaking, rinse.

RINSE THE BEANS THAT YOU'VE COOKED OR TAKEN OUT OF THE CAN. This can help remove excess undigestible elements in the legumes. Just put them in a colander or sieve and rinse under running water HOWEVER THERE'S ALWAYS AQUAFABA (see page 122 for the Vegan Mayonnaise Recipe).

Drain your legumes thoroughly too, because excess water will influence the consistency and flavor of your finished dip.

If you have the time and can be bothered, remove the outer coating or skins of the beans, since a lot of the anti-nutrients are stored in the skins. Obviously, this is easier said than done in many cases. If you squeeze a well-cooked broad bean (a.k.a. fava bean) its lovely green innards should just pop out of its skin. Mung bean skins practically fall off during vigorous cooking or rinsing. Good luck with getting the skin off a kidney bean though. I'll leave it up to you to decide how you want to play this one. In some cases, like with broad beans, you HAVE to do it. In other cases, it's probably not worth the effort.

You'll notice that many bean-based dip recipes contain cumin. This isn't just for flavor but also to aid digestibility. You can also add small amounts of asafoetida, fennel, ginger or turmeric to recipes that don't specify those spices as ingredients if you like the flavor because they also aid digestibility. You don't have to add much. You don't even have to be able to add enough to detect the taste of the spices. Just be aware that turmeric imparts a yellow coloring to your dip, which might or might not be what you want. In Central American and Mexican cooking a herb called epazote is used as a flavoring with a taste of slightly bitter lemon that also alleviates beany gassiness. If you can't get the fresh stuff, you can buy dried epazote in specialty Central and South American grocers and it naturally works well in Mexican dips but use it sparingly.

Similarly, even if the recipe doesn't call for it, you can add small amounts of seaweed (either dry or pre-soaked) to your dip like kelp, kombu or any number of other seaweeds that you can buy at health food stores and specialty Asian grocers. Once again, you only need tiny amounts a teaspoon or less to get some benefit of digestibility and added vitamins and minerals. If you're feeling adventurous though, adding enough seaweed will contribute a saltiness and an umami element to the dip, which you might like.

Some legumes are easier to digest than others. Adzuki beans and the small lentils used in dahls are relatively easy to digest, as are mung beans. In fact, mung beans can be used instead of the traditional chickpeas in hummus and work quite well.

Taking steps like thorough soaking and rinsing and adding the right spices or seaweeds should go far in alleviating some of the more embarrassing side effects of legumes. In the end, the way your body reacts to food is a highly personal thing and changes over time, so keep all of this in mind as you explore the wonderful world of legumes and the tasty dips that they can make.

… AND THERE ARE FROZEN LEGUMES TOO

Unlike canned legumes, frozen ones aren't usually salted or have any other additives. People vary in their opinions about frozen vegetables, but frozen legumes don't have to be soaked or cooked for hours. Preparation can be as minimal as blanching them in boiling water for several minutes. Frozen legumes are arguably better than fresh, dried or canned, because the freezing process breaks down the cellular structure of the bean and makes it easier to digest. Also, freezing preserves the sweet sugars in many beans before those sugars turn to starch through the process of ageing and drying or simply waiting on a shelf, waiting to be bought. Frozen legumes are, in fact, quite good for dips.

Not all legumes are available frozen. The most common ones that are, are:

Peas both full-sized and baby

Green beans both full-sized and baby

Broad or fava beans which you'll need to de-skin

Edamame which you'll need to take out of their pods

More rarely you can get a variety of green, white, yellow, pink, red, brown or black beans frozen too, as well as lentils and chickpeas. Specialty Asian or Middle Eastern supermarkets are often your best bets here.

In short, frozen beans that have been blanched for a few minutes in water, and then occasionally given a quick sauté in olive oil, can be substituted for the same bean that you've either cooked or taken from a can.

TWO FINAL BITS OF GOOD NEWS

Cooked legumes freeze well, so make up a big batch and what you don't use immediately can be frozen for months at a time. I suggest storing them in containers that hold 400 to 500 g (1 lb) of cooked legumes since this is an easy and convenient size to thaw and use.

If you eat legumes on a regular basis the side effects diminish substantially in most people after a couple of weeks. So, you'll be able to stand near naked flames again without risk of catastrophe.

THE FINE ART OF ROASTING, GRILL-ING AND CARAMELIZING VEGETABLES

Perhaps you're one of those unfortunates who grew up in a home where vegetables were just boiled and then served to you. If you were, you have my sincerest sympathies.

But to get the best out of many vegetables, especially the starchy ones used in dips, you need to caramelize. Caramelization is the process where through slow cooking and browning the boring bland starches in the vegetables break down and turn into delicious sweet sugars.

Caramelization is easy and the results are well worth the effort.

I don't know why they don't teach this stuff in schools.

The preparation methods below should each make about 500 g (1 lb) of finished vegetables.

Even if you don't use this much vegetable there are advantages to cooking this much at once.

Some dips require more cooked vegetable than others so at least you know that you'll have enough. You won't run out of your not-so-raw materials.

It takes around the same time to cook a large quantity as a small amount.

What you don't use, you can freeze and use in a number of different non-dip dishes and save the time later.

Eggplant / Aubergines

Use about 1 kilo (2 lb) of eggplant since they lose a lot of moisture in the cooking process. About 3 or 4 medium-sized eggplants should do the trick.

Wash the eggplants but don't bother drying them. Then use one of the following methods, whichever works best for you given your temperament and available equipment.

METHOD ONE GRILL

Take the whole eggplants and place them on a gas or coal barbecue grill on a medium low heat. Slowly char them. Charring happens when the skin turns from purple to beige, then to brown with black bits on it and then mostly black. This should take anywhere from 30 to 45 minutes …

OR

Cut the eggplants through their cross-sections into discs and cook until they're nicely grilled on both sides.

METHOD TWO BAKE

Cover a rimmed baking sheet in aluminium foil. Take the whole eggplants and place them on the sheet in a single layer and bake them in the oven until charred …

OR

Halve the eggplants and cover them in olive oil and place them on the baking sheet, cut sides up, in a single layer and bake them in the oven until charred on the skin.

Either way, this method should take up to 90 minutes.

My personal preference with either method is to cut the eggplants rather than leave them whole. That way at least some charring occurs on the exposed inner flesh. This gives the eggplant a smokier flavor which I rather like, but it's not to everyone's taste.

After the eggplants are cooked they should be completely tender. Test this by skewering them either at the top near the green stem or at their base. If you meet with any resistance at all, keep cooking. This process can't be rushed. You need time to develop the full flavor potential of the eggplant.

Once cooked, wrap the eggplants in foil and leave to rest for about 15 minutes. This will allow steam from the eggplants to loosen the skin.

Once the 15 minutes are up, remove the foil. If the eggplants are whole, cut them in half. Carefully scoop out the eggplant flesh with a spoon and set aside in a bowl. If you've cut the eggplant into discs, remove the skin. If there are any charred bits in the scooped-out flesh pick the bits out, or feel free to leave a little bit in if you like the charred flavor. Whatever you do, it's important that you remove the skin from the flesh. The skin's too tough to add any value to the finished dip.

Place the scooped-out flesh in a salad spinner and gently spin, removing any excess liquid. Discard excess liquid. This step might not be necessary if you've used the halved-eggplant baking technique.

Carrots and Parsnips

Cooking Time: 1 hour

Take about 600 g (1 1/2 lb) medium to large carrots (smaller carrots will dry out too much) and peel them. Alternatively, you can give them a little scrape with one of those forest-green plastic scouring pads that you normally use to clean non-stick frypans that have lost their non-stickiness.

If the carrots are very large then cut them in half, lengthwise.

The same principles apply to parsnips, but you don't have to peel them.

Cover a rimmed baking sheet in alfoil. Generously sprinkle the sheet with olive oil. Or use a spray olive oil and be equally generous. Take the carrots and place them on the sheet in a single layer then generously spritz them with more olive oil.

Bake the carrots in a very slow oven, no more than say, 140° C (275° F). There is no need to pre-heat the oven.

Now wait and be patient. This will take at least an hour, but all the while the carrot flavors will be maturing and sweetening. It's hard to give an exact time because ovens vary and so do carrots, but the secret here is the slow cooking.

You want the carrots to be super tender. This isn't an 'al dente' carrot for a Sunday roast. This is a carrot that you're going to puree for a dip or spread. Feel free to poke the carrot with a skewer or a fork. You won't have to worry about the hole marks because the carrots are going to get mashed anyway.

There's no need to turn the carrots at any stage either unless you're one of those compulsive neurotics like me who can't help themselves.

Once you're happy with the doneness of the carrots, they should be slightly browned on the outside. If they're not, crank up the oven to 230° C (450° F) and blast the carrots for about 5 minutes. This should finish things off nicely. Don't let the carrots burn!

NOTE:

Using this method the vegetables will often dry out slightly. This is perfectly normal because these vegetables produce a dryer mash that allows more control over the final texture of the dip.

YOU CAN USE THE EXACT SAME TECHNIQUE FOR THE FOLLOWING VEGETABLES, WITH THE FOLLOWING MODIFICATIONS.

Capsicum / Bell Peppers

Use about 600 g (1 1/4 lb) to allow for moisture loss. The capsicum is done when the skins peel of easily.

Alternately, use the method for cooking capsicum as outlined in the recipe for Harissa (page 141).

Courgettes / Zucchinis

Use about 1 kg (2 lb) because zucchinis have a lot of water.

No need to peel or scrape the skins. Cut the zucchinis in half lengthwise and bake skin side down. You'll usually use the zucchini with the skin.

Garlic

Cooking Time: At least 40 minutes but can go on for up to 90 minutes.

Many people who don't like garlic because they find it overpowering or too pungent or astringent, change their minds about this most excellent herb once they've tasted the roasted, caramelized version.

Position a rack in your oven so that it's in the centre of the oven.

Pre-heat your oven to 200°C (400°F). Fan forced is unnecessary.

Get a whole bulb of garlic.

Peel off the outer dry layers of skin; but keep the bulb intact so that the cloves are still attached to the base.

Slice the top off the bulb, so that the bulbs are a little exposed.

Repeat this until you have four or five bulbs prepared.

Place the bulbs on a sheet of alfoil.

Drizzle generously with olive oil (or use a spray) so that the tops of the garlic are covered in a thin layer of oil.

Wrap the bulbs in the foil, keeping the bases of the bulbs at the bottom of the foil and place the wrapped bulbs on a baking tray, then place the baking tray on the middle rack of the oven.

The garlic is done when it's lost its harsh, raw character and its aroma is sweeter and more complex. Longer oven time will brown the garlic and give it a smokier flavor.

Allow the garlic to cool in the foil. Moisture from the garlic will soften the skin so that it's easily removed.

While the garlic is cooled but not yet cold, you can remove the garlic from the skin. It'll be soft and creamy. Even like this, just on its own, it makes a delicious spread that you can have with toast. You can also use this pasty, caramelized garlic in any dip that requires garlic as an ingredient. Use the same quantity as you would of raw garlic.

Warning:

This process will fill your house with a heady garlic aroma. If you don't want that to happen I suggest that you open a few windows. And doors too maybe. And warn your neighbours, perhaps.

Bonus Tip: If you want to get rid of the garlic smell from an especially garlicky dip, there are a number of things you can do either individually or in combination to neutralize the odour from your breath:

eat a raw apple

chew fresh mint

chew fresh lettuce

drink some lemon juice, straight, swishing it around your teeth

gargle and drink some green tea.

OTHER VEGETABLES THAT YOU CAN USE THE GARLIC METHOD ON

Broccoli and cauliflower. Keep the broccoli and cauliflower florets as large and as whole as possible.

Brussel sprouts. If using large brussel sprouts, half them.

Fennel. If using large bulbs of fennel, cut them in half along their widest cross-section.

Use 500 g (2 pounds) of vegetable to produce roughly the same amount cooked, since water losses are minimal with these vegetables.

After the vegetables have become tender, open the foil and turn on the heat in the oven to maximum. Bake until you get some slight browning happening but don't let them burn.

Pumpkin

Use about 750 g (1 1/2 lb) of pumpkin to allow for moisture loss.

Cut the pumpkin into segments and scoop out the seeds and the seed pulp with a spoon. DO NOT PEEL THE SEGMENTS. Lay them on the baking tray skin side down so that the flesh is as exposed as possible to the oven heat without making contact with the tray. If the segments refuse to balance on their backs, then slice a little from their skin base to provide a flat surface for them to be stable. Cook until super tender and blast until the segments are slightly burned at the edges, if this hasn't already happened during the long cooking process. Wait until the pumpkin has cooled before peeling or cutting off the remaining skins.

Potato

600 g (1 1/4 lb) of unpeeled potato should yield about 500 g (1 lb) of the finished product.

Use the same technique as for pumpkin. Do not peel the potatoes. Halve and bake skin side down. Use a potato variety that's good for baking. Since there are literally thousands of potato types and not all potatoes are available in all regions, just ask your local grocer to recommend some. Supermarkets are also getting better at labelling which potato is best for what but don't be afraid to ask someone with local knowledge.

Sweet Potato/Yams/Kumara/Beetroot

600 g (1 1/4 lb) of unpeeled vegetable should yield about 500 g (1 lb) of the finished product.

Sweet potato, yams and kumara are actually different vegetables and what you call them depends on where they're from and where you're from. However, they cook in very similar ways. The method is the same as for pumpkin. Halve them and bake them skin side down.

Mushrooms

You'll need about 2 kg (4 1/2 lb) of mushrooms to produce 500 g (1 lb) of finished, cooked product because the water content of mushrooms is so high.

Although not technically a vegetable only pedants like me care about the botanical status of mushrooms, which are actually fungi and belong to a whole other kingdom of life, being neither animal or plant.

The most common types of mushrooms are the ever-versatile white button mushroom and the more robustly-flavored Swiss brown. Whichever you use, cut them into medium slices. Put a generous amount of butter into a large pan. Cast iron is best for this. Yes, you can use oil or margarine or even a mixture of cooking fats, but butter in this case really is better.

Over a low heat, slowly sauté the mushrooms stirring with a wooden spoon as they brown. This process cannot be rushed and unless you're predisposed to going into some sort of meditative trance it's best if you do your mushroom sautéing while you're doing something else, stirring every now and then so that the mushrooms on the bottom of the pan don't burn. Because you're doing this on a low heat it's unlikely that the mushrooms or the butter will burn unless you get distracted. So, don't get distracted.

From time to time you might want to add a tablespoon of water to loosen up any bits that have stuck to the bottom of the pan. You don't want to lose those flavors.

Onions

to 1 hour, depending on method used.

You'll need about 1.5 kg (3 lb) of medium thin sliced onion to produce 500 g (1 lb) of finished, cooked product because the water content of onions is relatively high.

The best onions for caramelization are brown or yellow onions. They develop a more complex and deep sweetness that white onions and the delicate essences of purple or Spanish onions, although sweeter when raw, don't survive the cooking process very well. The other problem with purple onions is that when cooked, their color goes a sort of vomit green, so … not great.

Use the same technique as for mushrooms (above) but in this case use oil with maybe just a small knob of butter added. This process cannot be rushed. Long and slow is the way for perfectly caramelized onions. Use a medium heat on the hob.

You'll notice as you go that there will be brown bits sticking to the bottom of the pan. These are browned sugars that have come from the body of the onion, feel free to pour in a couple of tablespoons of water into the pan and loosen those flavor-filled sugars away. This process is known as deglazing. The water will evaporate anyway and the sugars will concentrate even further.

If you're feeling adventurous add about ¼ teaspoon of baking soda (but no more and only once!) to the deglazing water for this amount of onion in order to increase the caramelization.

If you feel that the onions aren't browning enough, stick a cooking thermometer into them and check their temperature. Caramelization in onions starts at the 110°C (230°F) mark, which is easily achievable so if this isn't happening you've got the heat on a little too low.

You can also caramelize onions in the same way as garlic (above) and it takes about the same time as the garlic. It will give you a different, but equally delicious result than from pan caramelization.

Infusions

Olive oil is popular because it's super versatile. It can be used both hot as a cooking oil and cold as a salad or dipping oil.

One way to showcase its versatility is to infuse the oil with herbs or spices.

Take a clean bottle and add the herbs or spices first. A couple of tablespoons per 500 ml (1 pint) is plenty. Or for a more spectacular touch, a whole sprig of herb. Rosemary and bay leaves are perennial favorites. Make sure though that the herb or spice is **quite dry** before you put it in the oil, as any latent water or moisture will tend to ferment and spoil the oil. This is especially important if you're using garlic, onion or chili to flavor your oil. Dried mushroom slices also work well. After a week or so of infusion, you should really be able to note the difference as the essential oil from the herb or spice has permeated and dissolved into the carrier olive oil.

Feel free then to use the infused oil as a finishing oil for your dips.

Quick and Dirty

There's one more source of deliciously-flavored oils that people often ignore. These days it's fairly easy to buy jars of preserved vegetables in oil that people use in antipasto. These include:

◊ artichoke hearts

◊ charred or grilled capsicum / bell peppers

◊   charred or grilled courgettes / zucchinis

◊   charred or grilled eggplant / aubergines

◊   mushrooms

◊   dried or semi-dried tomatoes.

Usually people just eat the vegetables and then throw out the oil, but this is an incredible waste. Those veggies have usually been sitting in that oil for weeks, if not months. All the while they've been imparting the oils that they've been bathing in with their essences, scents and flavors. The result is that all that deliciousness is now in the oil too. So, drain away any watery juice, rebottle the oil and keep it and use it as a finishing oil for your dips, or as dipping oils (mixed with balsamic vinegar and herbs) in their own right. These oils are strongly flavored, so use them judiciously. If they're too strong, dilute them with a light olive oil.

These oils will keep for ages if you freeze them. Just thaw them out as you need them. Simple.

ROASTING NUTS AND SEEDS

An important point to note is that seeds and nuts are a plant's way of having babies. It's not in the interest of a plant to have its babies eaten, so plants have developed ways of defending their seeds from consumption. One way is to protect the seed with a tough outer shell. But you can crack a shell. Then there's an inner seed coating or hull that protects the seed from digestion. This form of protection falls apart when the seed or nut is ground up. But there's another trick up the seed's sleeve. Seeds often contain chemicals called dietary inhibitors or anti-nutrients. These chemicals make the seed less useful as food because the anti-nutrients block your body from being able to use the vitamins, minerals and other goodness in the seed.

The good news is that in many cases these anti-nutrients can be significantly reduced through some form of cooking. While it might sound as if a 'raw' nut butter is better because it's more 'natural' it's often a good idea, when dealing with seeds, to roast the seeds first before grinding them into butters. Of course, there's nothing stopping you from blending raw nuts with roasted nuts in a butter in order to experience different types of flavors too, but in the interest of nutrition the digestibility of a roasted nut or seed generally makes up for any nutrition that might be lost in the roasting process.

How to Roast Your Seeds

There are several ways of roasting nuts and seeds. Pick whichever works for you depending on your available equipment, time and personality.

BIG WARNINGS:

Always roast ONE type of seed or nut at a time. Nuts vary quite a bit in their cooking time because of their different sizes and oil types. Mixing your seeds or nuts for roasting is pretty much a recipe for disaster. Use unsalted raw nuts and seeds for roasting so that you can control how much salt you add later.

Some nuts like peanuts, hazelnuts and pecans have a definite skin which sheds during roasting. It's best to get rid of this skin before processing. The quick way to do this is to take the tray outside so you don't make a mess. Place the nuts in a tea towel. Rub the nuts through the tea towel then open the towel up, exposing the nuts and the skins, and blow the dried skin away.

When roasting or dry frying nuts for use in nut butters it's best to go light. Over-roasting results in a dry nut that doesn't release as much oil, which means you have to add oil, which is something that you'll want to avoid.

Dry Roasting in a Pan

You'll get the best results for this if you have a cast iron pan, but a stainless-steel one will do too. DO NOT ADD OIL TO THE PAN.

Over a low heat gently heat your WHOLE nuts or seeds, stirring continually with a wooden spoon. Over several minutes the oil in the seeds gradually heats up, essentially frying the seeds and nuts from the inside.

Pay attention to the color of the seeds. It's up to you to decide if you want a light or dark roast, but a light roast is better for nut butters.

Pay attention to the smell of the seeds. You want them to lose their raw smell, but you will want to take them off the heat before they cook any further beyond that.

In some cases, some seeds, like sesame seeds, pumpkin seeds or sunflower seeds begin to pop. At this point take the pan off the heat and pour the seeds immediately into a bowl (preferably a stainless one because it dissipates heat quickly).

Even when taken off the heat, latent heat in the seeds or nuts will continue to cook them, so it's best to take the seeds off the flame and out of the pan before they're quite done so that they don't burn. Once in their bowl, continue to stir to cool the seeds down as quickly as possible.

Oven Roasting

If you're doing a large quantity of nuts, oven roasting is more efficient.

Preheat your oven to 190° C (375°F).

On a baking tray lined with alfoil, spread a single layer of nuts.

Table of Oven Roasting Times for Seeds and Nuts

5 10 minutes	Pine nuts, pepitas (pumpkin seeds), sesame seeds, sunflower seeds

(Having said this, I still prefer dry frying seeds in a pan. Because seeds are much smaller than nuts, the line between roasting and burning is really fine, so roasting seeds requires a light touch and a bit of either experience or obsessive compulsion).

7-10 minutes	Almonds and pistachios
10-15 minutes	Pecans and walnuts
12-15 minutes	Hazelnuts and macadamias
15-20 minutes	Peanuts in shell
20-25 minutes	Shelled peanuts
25 minutes	Chestnuts

NOTE:

Everyone's oven is different, and nuts vary from season to season. Err on the side of caution and set your timer to the low end of the estimated roasting time for the oven.

Another option that you might like to try when roasting nuts and seeds is using an air-fryer. All air-fryers are different so follow the manufacturer's instruction on their use. It might take some experimentation to get this right so err on the side of caution and lower temperatures and shorter cooking times until you get the results you like.

Acknowledgements and Thanks

Thanks to the team at New Holland for all their help turning my dream books into physical realities.

Thanks also to TAFE NSW and the Government of Australia for supporting my studies in so many ways, like the way that the library staff of Wentworth Falls TAFE Glenda Pryor, Michael Hart, Sue Pears and Lesley Smith always do that little bit extra to find me the right book for my research; or the way that the support staff in the Hospitality department - Annette Troy, Angela Anderson and Daniel Silk - were always so helpful finding me the right ingredients, equipment and resources when I needed them; and to the Administrative and Customer Service staff, those usually unsung heroes who make navigating the bureaucracy of vocational education somewhat more painless Genevieve Bernard, Gillian Cowie, Maria Dege, Isabella Jaworski and Helen Simpson.

Effusive thanks to Mon Chef Amar Mall and to Ma Cheffe Angelique Zielinski as well as hospitality teachers Kirralee Burt, Matthew Fletcher and Karen Helmrich, head teachers Wendy Ashcroft-Ware and John Rankins for their guidance and indulgence during the years that I formally studied commercial cookery and table service. Believe me, if you're teaching me you *need* to be indulgent. Thanks to my fellow full-time students who completed the course with me too Barbara, Charlie, Gigi, Jade, Nate and Wilhelm. Thanks to all of you for giving me one on the most gratifying educational experiences of my life.

First published in 2019 by New Holland Publishers
London • Sydney • Auckland

Bentinck House, 3–8 Bolsover Street, London W1W 6AB, UK
1/66 Gibbes Street, Chatswood, NSW 2067, Australia
5/39 Woodside Ave, Northcote, Auckland 0627, New Zealand

newhollandpublishers.com

A record of this book is held at the British Library and the
National Library of Australia.

ISBN 9781760790493

Group Managing Director: Fiona Schultz
Publisher: Fiona Schultz
Project Editor: Elise James
Designer: Yolanda La Gorcé
Production Director: Arlene Gippert
Printer: Toppan Leefung Printing Limited

10 9 8 7 6 5 4 3 2 1

Keep up with New Holland Publishers on Facebook
facebook.com/NewHollandPublishers